KEY STAGE 2

HEADTEACHER'S AWARD

Revision for CURRICULUM TESTS AND PRACTICE PAPERS

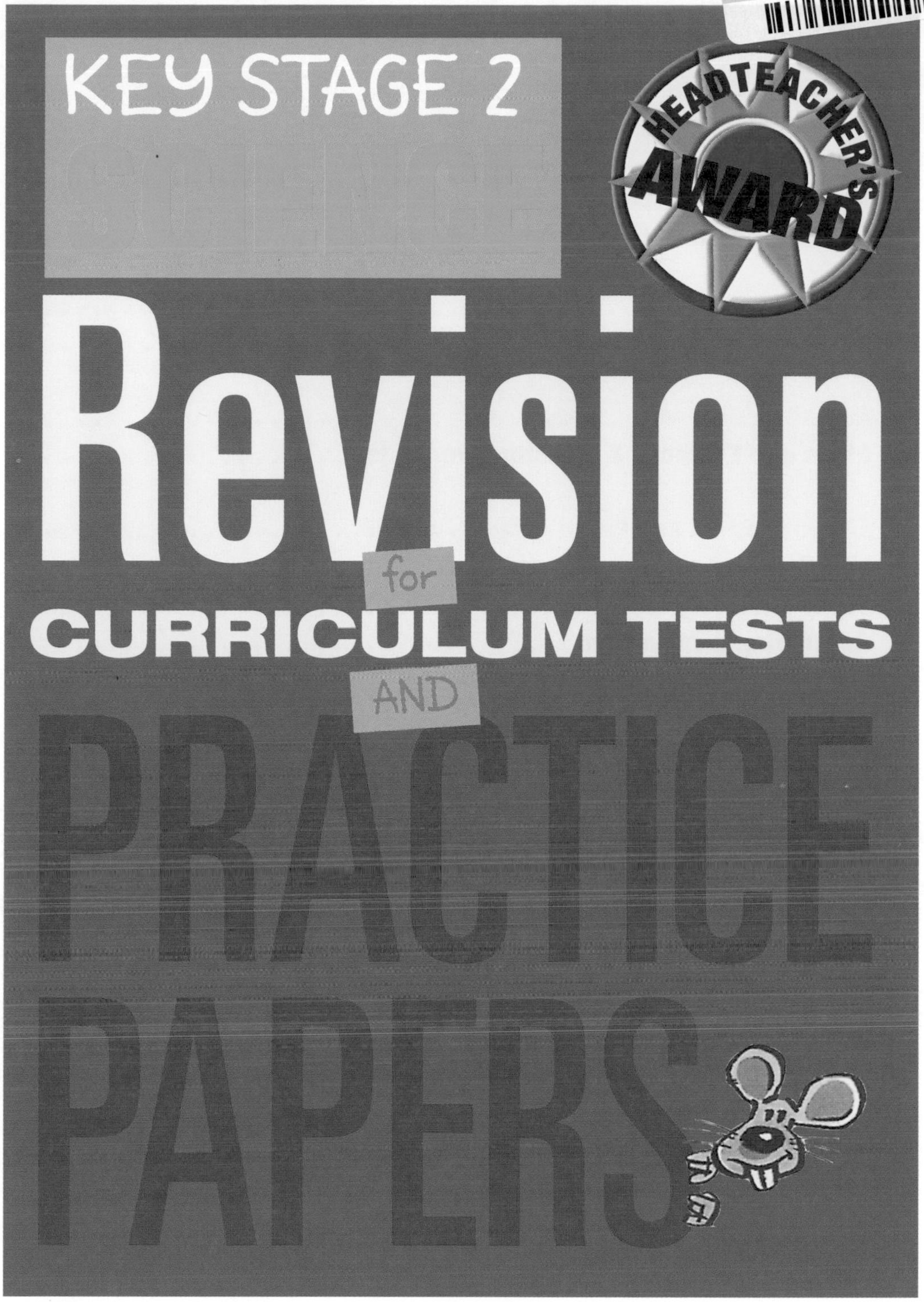

Author
Camilla de la Bédoyère

Consultant Editor
Christine Warwick

This is a Flame Tree Book
First published in 2002

02 03 04 05

10 9 8 7 6 5 4 3 2 1

ISBN 1-903817-69-2

Flame Tree is part of
The Foundry Creative Media Company Ltd
Crabtree Hall, Crabtree Lane, Fulham,
London SW6 6TY

Visit the Foundry website: www.foundry.co.uk/flametree

Thanks to Dave Jones for the technical illustrations.
Thanks also to Jenny Bishop, Lucy Bradbury, Vicky Garrard, Chris Herbert, Julia Rolf, Graham Stride, Nick Wells, Polly Willis and Tom Worsley.

A copy of the CIP data for
this book is available from the British Library.

Printed in Croatia

Contents

Foreword

In today's ever-changing educational climate in which targets, levels of achievement and school league-tables grab headline news, it is important to remember what is at the core of it all: the education of your child.

Children learn at different speeds and achieve different levels during their early years at school, so it is important that a child is encouraged to work to the best of his or her ability, whatever their standard.

The Head Teacher Awards, which many schools use, is a simple, yet highly effective way to motivate children. In the classroom a child may be given an HTA for a particularly good piece of work, or for trying hard in a subject they may struggle with, or for neat handwriting, fluent reading, or imaginative creative writing. The list is endless, yet the effect of the HTA on the child is great: they feel valued and that something they have really tried hard at has been noticed.

The idea behind the Head Teacher's Award Series is much the same as the award-scheme practised in the classroom. This book has been devised for use by children who are coming up to their National Tests at the end of Key Stage Two. Not only does it reinforce all the information they need to know for their Tests through a series of fun and practical questions and activities, it gives children a chance to work a little harder and be rewarded with a Head Teacher's Award. Throughout the book, one or two questions on each page have a HTA symbol next to them, indicating that that particular question or activity may require a little more work or a more lateral approach in order to get the answer right. It is up to the parent to decide what the award should be (we are not advocating bribery here!), something to make the child feel they have reached a target. It may be that you decide with your child that they have to get a certain number of HTAs in the book before they can have their 'award', based on their ability.

Written by teachers of Key Stage Two children, the aim of this book is that through a combination of revision, motivational aids and practical tests that the child can take in a familiar and comfortable environment, they will be as prepared as they can be for the National Tests that they will take at the end of Key Stage Two.

John Foster

Former Head Teacher of St Marks Junior School, Salisbury.

HEADTEACHER'S AWARD

Introduction

What are SATs?

Children who are in Years 3 to 6 study Key Stage 2 of the National Curriculum. At the end of Year 6, in May, the children are tested on their knowledge and skills in three core subjects: mathematics, English and science. The tests are commonly known as SATs, which stands for Standard Assessment Tasks, or NCTs (National Curriculum Tests). The teachers use the SATs results, as well as continuous assessment that is conducted in the classroom, to assess how well the children are doing.

How This Book Works

By the time your child takes their SATs they should have covered everything in the National Curriculum that they are meant to know. This book is not intended to teach new subjects in science, but should be used as an aid to revision and improving exam technique. The book is divided into two main sections:

Revision Section

The essentials of the science curriculum are covered with clear explanations and examples. On the pages you will find key words or concepts highlighted to help your child remember them.

Parent's Guides

These feature regularly throughout the book and may:

- **Explain why a topic is important.**
- **Suggest what you can do to reinforce your child's learning of a topic.**
- **Give examples of activities you can do together.**

Questions

Quick questions feature throughout the book. By answering the questions your child will reinforce the concepts they have just covered in the text. Answering the questions correctly gives the children confidence and motivates them to continue working their way through the book.

Head Teacher's Award

Throughout the book Head Teacher Award Questions (HTAs) feature. These are slightly harder than the other questions: achieving a high standard in answering Head Teacher's Award Question earns your child the HTA.

Practice Papers

This is the section where your child can practise using the skills they have revised. There are three practice papers, including a Level 6 extension. These are explained in more detail on page 38. Answers and a marking scheme are included.

What You Can Do to Help

Encourage your child to complete the questions and activities that are included in the revision section. Practice really consolidates learning and will be greatly beneficial to your child. Answering questions together will also help you identify any particular difficulties your child is having.

Promote good learning habits. Encourage your child to plan their revision, allowing plenty of time for breaks. They will learn and retain more in two periods of 20 minutes with a five-minute break than an unbroken 45 minute period. Teach them to revisit a topic regularly, so that it becomes part of their long-term memory.

Motivate your child to succeed. Reward your child for every HTA they get – discuss this with your child to agree a suitable reward.

A healthy body keeps a mind active. Ensure that your child eats a well-balanced and healthy diet, gets plenty of exercise and a full night's sleep every night.

Keep the tests in perspective. Remember that SATs are as much a test of the school's success as of your child's ability, so do not cause your child anxiety by over-stressing the importance of the exams. Nor are SATs an end in themselves: they are part of a whole process designed to ensure that your child has a solid foundation for later learning and success.

Ideas in Science

Science – What's the Point?

- We learn about the world around us
- We find ways to make life better for ourselves and others
- We learn new ways of thinking
- We learn to question things
- We learn how to look for evidence to support ideas.

Questions

1. Do beetles have bones?
2. Is the Moon a planet?
3. What gas do we breathe?

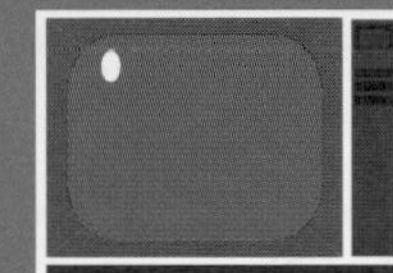

Activity

Using books or the Internet, investigate the invention of the television. When was it invented and by whom? What would you like to invent?

Science – What Has it Ever Done for Us?

Galileo Galiliei, a great Italian scientist, proved in the seventeenth century that the Earth is not the centre of the Universe and that it revolves around the Sun.

Edward Jenner, an English scientist of the nineteenth century, produced a vaccine to prevent smallpox. This was a terrible disease that disfigured or killed the people who caught it.

Thomas Edison, an American, was one of the world's greatest inventors. He helped to develop the modern electrical age and his work contributed greatly to the film, recording and telephone industries.

These are just a few examples of the contribution science has made to our lives. There are millions more – just look around you.

Science – How Do We Do It?

There are two main skills to science: thinking and discovering.

Parent's Guide

Through science children learn to question the world around them. They ask questions about things and carry out experiments to test their ideas. They learn how to be objective and how to evaluate evidence – important skills they can use in all areas of life.

Investigating in Science

Investigation is all about discovery. If you want to discover something you have to carry out an experiment.

An experiment:

Has an aim

- **What are you trying to find out?**
- **Which dissolves faster in warm water, salt or sugar?**

Is fair

- **You need to make sure that the water is the same temperature in both mugs.**

Is measurable

- **You need to be able to compare results. So you would use a clock to time how long the substances took to dissolve and then compare those times.**

During your experiment you need to record:

- **How you carried it out**
- **How you made your measurements**
- **Your results**

Results can be presented in various ways:

- **Tables**
- **Graphs**
- **Charts**

At the end of your experiment you need to draw a conclusion:

- **What did you learn?**
- **How could your experiment have been improved?**

Questions

Look at this chart. Salt was dissolved in water of different temperatures.

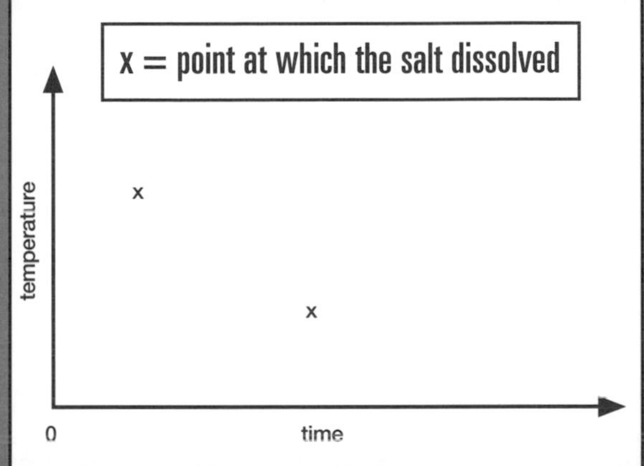

1. Salt dissolves faster in hotter water. True or false?

2. This is a bar graph. True or false?

3. This experiment could be repeated using sugar instead of salt. True or false?

Activity

With an adult's help, carry out the above experiment. Check that you use the same amount of salt and water each time and that you use the same cup or jug to measure the salt and water in each time. How will you measure the temperature of your water?

Living Things

Dead or Alive?

Some things are alive, e.g. you!

Some things are dead now, but were alive, e.g. this paper is made from trees that once lived.

Some things have never lived, and never will, e.g. the staple that holds this book together.

Living things, or things that once lived are called organisms and they are made-up of cells. Cells are very small and you need a microscope to see them. Think of them like building blocks – you use different types and sizes of building blocks when you build and there are lots of different types of cells, too. Plant cells are quite different to animal cells.

Remember

Organism is a word used to describe anything that lives, or has lived. It can be used for an animal or a plant, or other living things such as bacteria.

Questions

1. Draw circles around the items that are made of cells:

wood	plastic	feathers	glass
cement	rubber	flour	silver

Activity

Before you look at the next page, see if can think of any of the Seven Life Processes. No peeking!

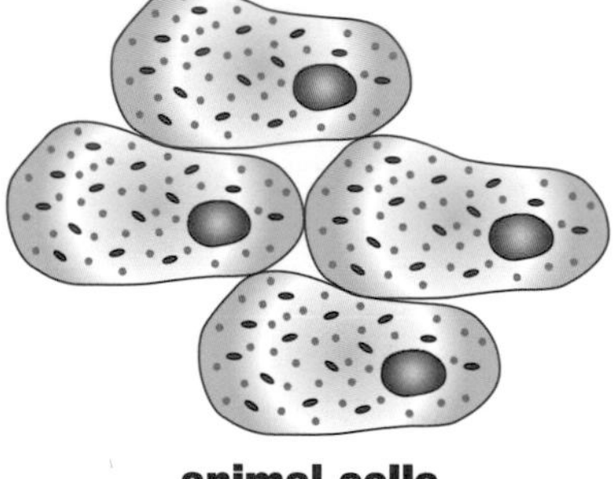

animal cells

plant cells

There are seven things that all living organisms do. They are called the Seven Life Processes.

Parent's Guide

It will help your child to learn the Seven Life Processes by heart. Talk about what each term means and how the processes differ for various organisms. Look in the library or on the Internet for photographs of cells.

The Seven Life Processes

All living organisms have the following things in common:

Move
Plants move towards the light; animals usually move their whole bodies.

Reproduce
We have babies, cats have kittens and plants produce seeds that grow into new plants.

Sensitive
We respond to things – prick your finger and you will jump; plants respond to light and grow towards it.

Nutrition
We get energy by eating food and plants make their own food using sunlight.

Excrete
We get rid of our bodies' waste products; plants get rid of waste gases.

Respire
Plants and animals use gases to change food into energy.

Grow
Baby elephants grow into huge elephants, acorns grow into enormous oak trees.

Questions

1. In what way are plants and animals similar?
2. In what ways do they differ?
3. What microscopic things are living organisms made up of?

Activity

It's hard to remember the Seven Life Processes, so think of a mnemonic to help you. This is a word or sentence made up of the first letter of each of the words you want to remember.

Animals and Plants – What's the Difference?

Animals	Plants
Communicate with one another	Do not communicate
Eat food to get energy	Use sunlight to make their own food
May move quickly	Move slowly
Stop growing at adulthood	Keep growing

Teeth

Humans and some animals have teeth to tear and crush food. The type of teeth an animal has depends on the kind of food it has to eat. Meat-eaters need sharp teeth to tear flesh. Plant-eaters need grinding teeth to break down their food, which is very tough.

Humans have:

1. **Incisors: front teeth that are sharp for cutting food.**
2. **Canines (fangs): for grabbing food (these teeth are big in hunting animals, like tigers or wolves).**
3. **Molars: for grinding and chewing food**

3. 2. 1.

Humans have two sets of teeth – 20 milk teeth and 32 (usually) permanent teeth.

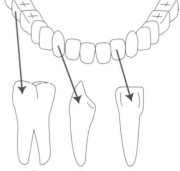

Looking After Your Teeth

The bacteria that live in your mouth can destroy the outside of a tooth, the enamel. The bad news is that these bacteria feed on sugary things. That's why fizzy drinks, sweets and chocolate-covered cereals can lead to tooth decay – and that means fillings.

To take care of your teeth you should:

- **Brush your teeth properly twice a day.**
- **Drink water or milk.**
- **Eat well; avoid sugary foods and drinks.**
- **Visit a dentist twice a year.**

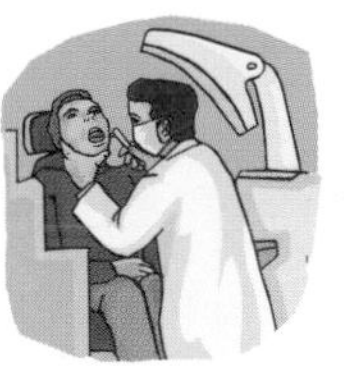

Questions

1. Name an animal that has fangs.

2. Name an animal that eats grass.

3. An elephant's tusks are teeth. True or false?

Activity

Use a dictionary to discover the meanings of these words:

Omnivore

Carnivore

Herbivore

Did You Know?

The Great White Shark can grow new teeth all its life?

Parent's Guide

The National Curriculum states that children need to learn the importance of an adequate and varied diet for health. Let your child help you make decisions about the family's meals. They can check that all the essential nutrients are included in the week's menu.

Healthy Eating

Eating well is one way of keeping yourself healthy. What you eat is called your 'diet'. A diet is not just something people follow to lose weight.

A good diet will enable your body and brain to grow and function (work) properly. A good diet will have a mixture of foods in it – it will be balanced. Remember that no food is bad for you as long as you don't have too much of it. The important word is balance.

Questions

1. Which is the healthiest drink – cola or milk?
2. Which ingredient in food causes tooth decay?
3. Is it healthy to eat a lot of fat?

Activity

Look at the ingredient lists on breakfast cereal boxes at the supermarket. Some of the 'healthy cereals for kids' are up to 40% sugar. Is that healthy? Which cereal has the most sugar in it? Which one has the least amount of sugar?

Food Groups	What They Do	Where You Find Them
Carbohydrates	For energy	Pasta, bread, cakes, rice
Proteins	For growth	Fish, eggs, meat, milk
Fats	For energy and brain growth	oil, butter, meat, milk, cheese
Fibre	To help your digestive system work properly	fruit, vegetables, whole-grain cereals
Vitamins and Minerals	For overall health	Fruit, vegetables, milk, cheese, eggs, meat, fish
Water	70% of your body is water	It comes out of a tap!

Blood and Circulation

The circulation system is the system that transports blood around your body.

The heart is a pump that sends blood around the body.

Blood is pumped to the lungs where it collects oxygen – a gas our bodies need.

Blood travels through vessels. There are three types of vessels:
- **Arteries carry blood with oxygen to parts of the body.**
- **Veins carry blood back to the lungs to get more oxygen.**
- **Capillaries are the tiny vessels that take food and oxygen to and from the cells.**

Blood is made up of cells.

White blood cells fight disease

Red blood cells carry oxygen

Platelets form scabs when you cut yourself

Plasma is the liquid that carries the cells

Questions

True or false?

1. Blood carries oxygen.

2. When you bleed red blood cells form a scab.

Activity

Find out why it is important that we have iron in our diets. Hint: it's something to do with blood.

Pulse

Blood that travels in veins is not carrying oxygen and it looks blue. Look at the underside of your wrist. Can you see the blue veins? Put your fingers over the veins and press gently. Can you feel a beating? This is your pulse and it shows you how hard your heart is beating to pump blood around your body.

Parent's Guide

Help your child devise an experiment to discover how exercise affects pulse rate. You will need a watch with a second hand. Draw up a table together to show the results. What conclusions can your child draw from this experiment?

Movement

Movement is possible because of two things:

- **A skeleton**
- **Muscles**

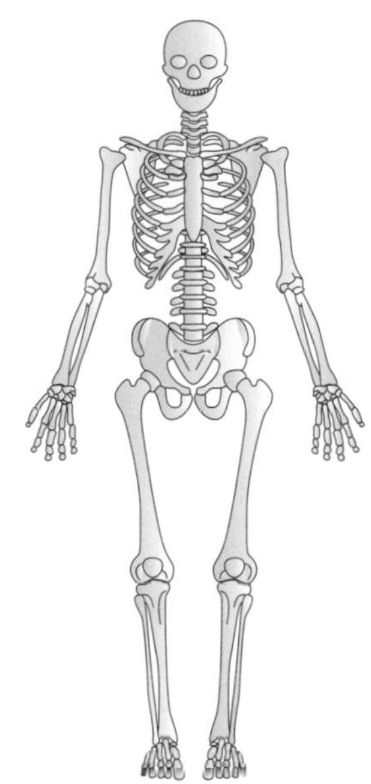

Skeletons

Skeletons are made of bones that are very strong but not too heavy. They can move because they have joints. Bend your arm, swing it around and flip your hand backwards and forwards. You are making your joints bend in all sorts of ways!

Skeletons are useful for the following reasons:

- **They support your body – you would be like a lump of jelly without one.**
- **They protect delicate parts of your body, such as your heart and brain.**
- **They move and muscles are attached to them**

Muscles

When muscles are contracted they get shorter. Bend your arms to show your muscles. As the biceps – the big muscles at the top – contract, they bulge and pull your arm bones upwards. Straighten your arms again; this time the muscles underneath your arms – the triceps – contract and the biceps relax.

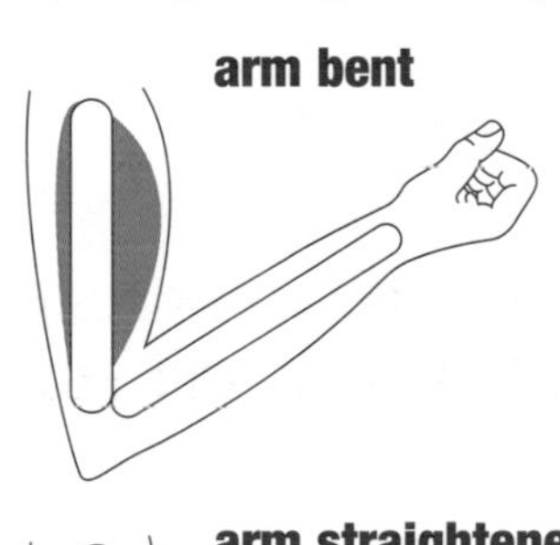

Questions

1. Which part of the skeleton protects the brain?

2. What do ribs protect?

3. Muscles often work in pairs. One contracts while the other relaxes. True or false?

Activity

Find out how many bones there are in the human body. How many bones do we have in just one foot? Where is the smallest bone found and what is called?

Reproduction

Reproduction means having babies (or puppies, if you are a dog!).

In humans, as in most animals, reproduction happens when a special cell from a female (woman) joins up with a special cell from a male (man).

The woman's special cell is called an egg and the man's special cell is called a sperm.

This 'joining-up' is called fertilisation or conception. We say that a baby has been conceived.

Once fertilisation occurs, the joined-up cells begin to grow and they are called an embryo. The embryo develops into a baby inside the mother.

Questions

1. What can a toddler do that a baby can't?

2. What is fertilisation?

Activity

Draw your own life cycle of a human. Write down the changes that people undergo as they age.

Did You Know?

The gestation period for an elephant is 22 months.

The place the baby grows is called a womb. The baby gets everything it needs to develop properly from its mother, through a special part of the womb called the placenta.

From conception to birth takes nine months. This time is known as gestation or pregnancy.

The Human Life Cycle

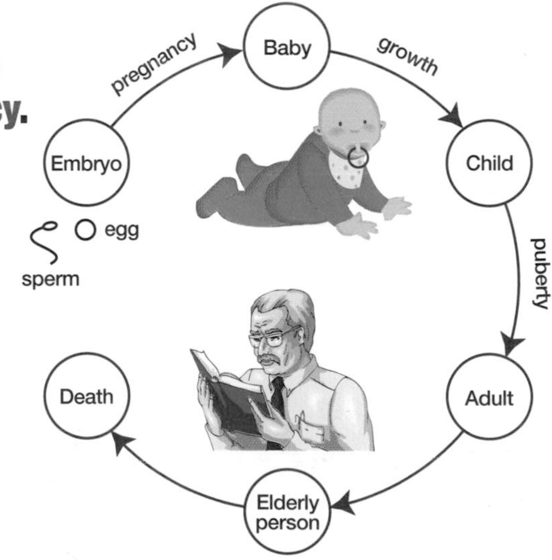

Remember

Puberty is the time when children change into adults.

Parent's Guide

Help your child with the drawing of a life-cycle and talk about the physical and mental changes that occur as people get older, as well as the new skills they develop through childhood. Your child may have more questions about puberty - there are plenty of books available to help you answer them.

Keeping Healthy

There are lots of things you can do to keep yourself healthy.

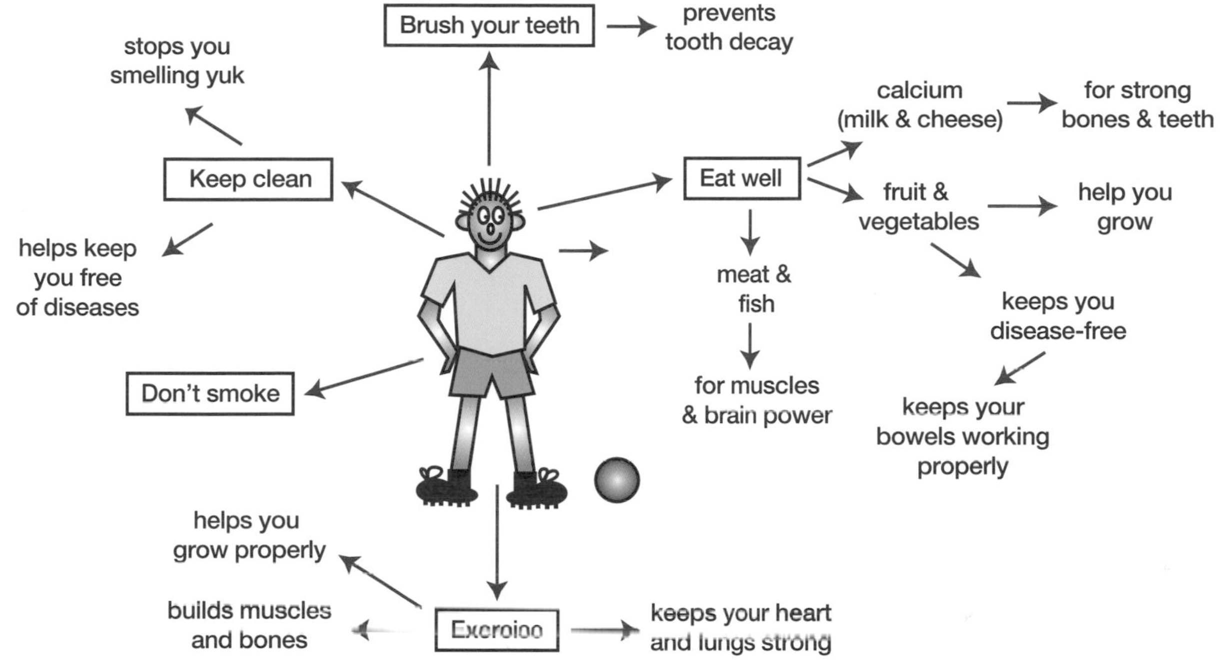

There are some things you should not do if you want to stay healthy.

- **Do not smoke – tobacco causes heart disease and lung cancer. Smoking also makes you smell.**
- **Do not drink alcohol – alcohol is a drug. It can be dangerous in large amounts.**
- **Adults should only drink alcohol in small amounts.**
- **Do not take drugs – they may damage your brain and many are addictive. This means you keep wanting more and more.**

Questions

True or false?

1. Smoking won't harm you if you give up when you are 40.

2. Exercise isn't necessary as long as you eat properly.

3. You can eat as much sugar as you like, as long as you brush your teeth.

Activity

Find out why vitamin C is important for good health. Which foods contain vitamin C?

Parts of a Plant

Plants, like animals, experience the Seven Life Processes. Look back to page 9 if you need a reminder of what they are.

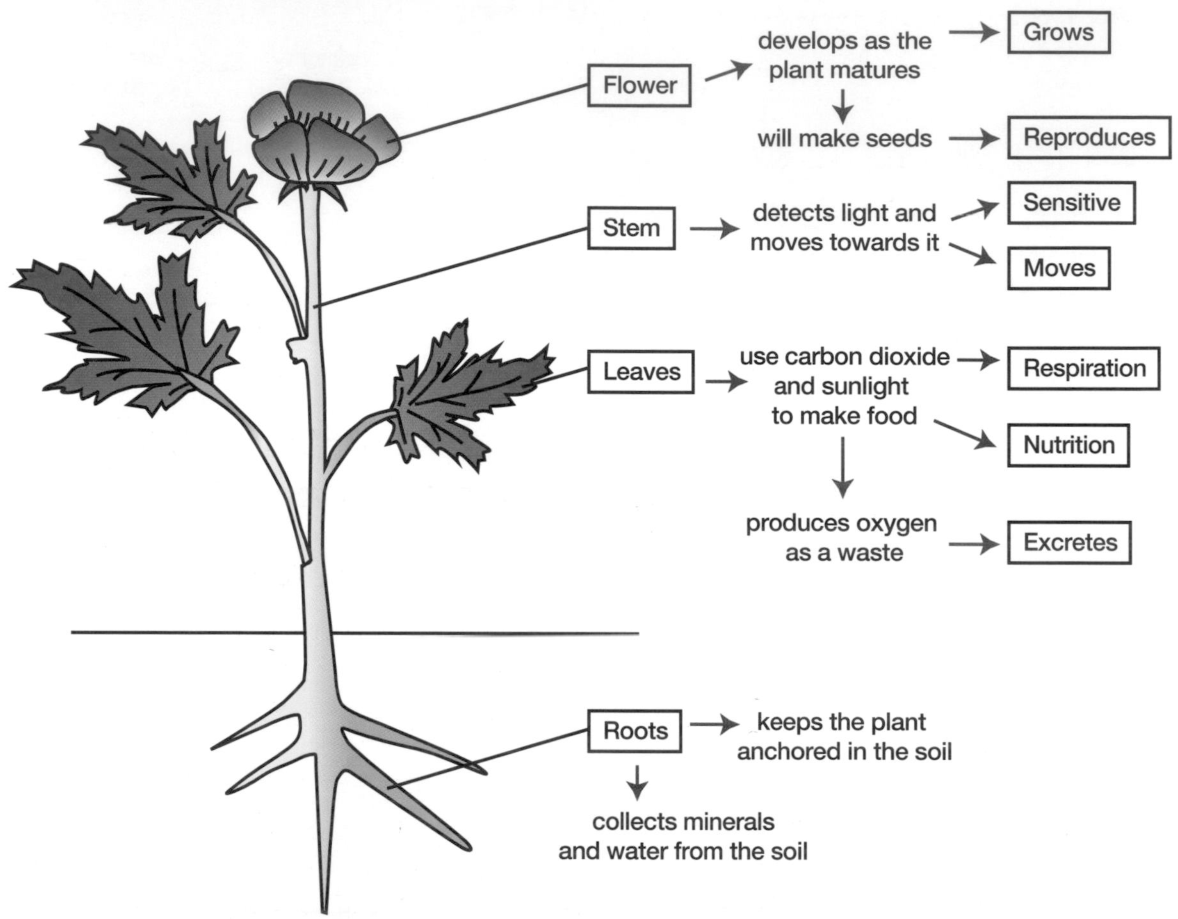

Questions

1. Which part of the plant is used in reproduction?
2. What are the leaves for?
3. Why do plants have roots?

Activity

Look at the picture on this page very carefully. Close the book and try to draw the picture yourself, putting in as many labels as you can remember.

Parent's Guide

It is important that your child has a clear understanding of the parts of a plant and what their functions are. Reinforce their learning by looking at real plants and testing each other on the names and jobs of their parts.

Nutrition

Animals eat food but plants make their own.

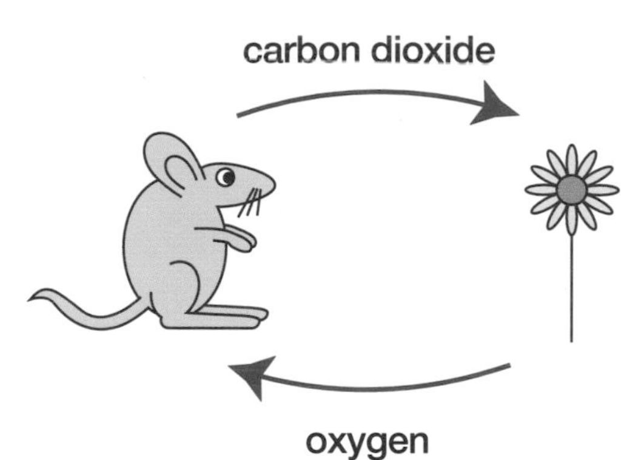

Plants make their food using water, carbon dioxide and the energy from sunlight.

This process is called photosynthesis.

The green stuff in leaves, chlorophyll, makes photosynthesis happen.

A waste product of photosynthesis is oxygen gas.

Remember

Carbon dioxide is the gas that animals breathe out. Oxygen is the gas that animals breathe in.

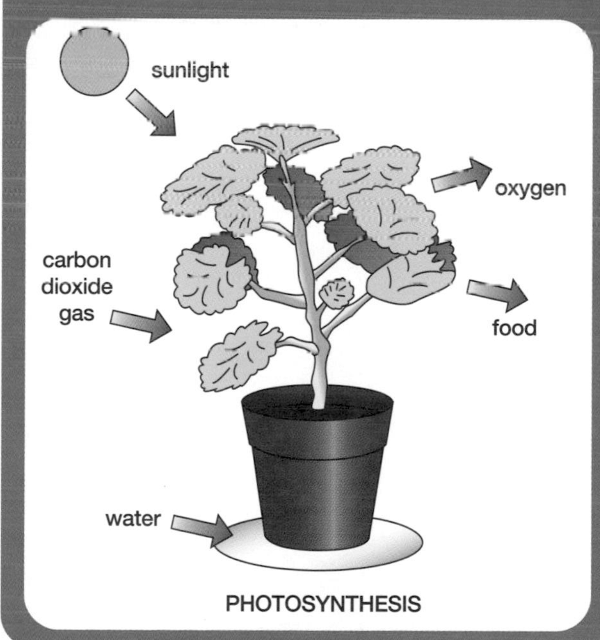

PHOTOSYNTHESIS

Sunlight + water + carbon dioxide = food + oxygen

Remember

Plants do not eat food – they make their own food by photosynthesis.
Plants need sunlight, water and carbon dioxide for photosynthesis.

Questions

1. What would happen to a pot plant if:
   a) You put it in a cupboard for several months, but still watered it?

   b) You put it in the sunlight but never watered it?

2. What gas do plants excrete?

Activity

We have learnt that plants need carbon dioxide and excrete oxygen, a gas that animals need. Can you describe why the tropical rainforests are known as 'the lungs of the planet'?

Plant Reproduction

- **Plants reproduce by producing seeds, which grow into new plants.**
- **The parts of the plant that make the seeds are in the flower.**
- **There are male parts and female parts within one flower.**

Questions

1. What is pollination?
2. Is the ovary a female or male part of a flower?

Activity

Copy the picture of Parts of a Flower. You may find it easier to trace. Make sure you put all of the labels in.

Parts of a Flower

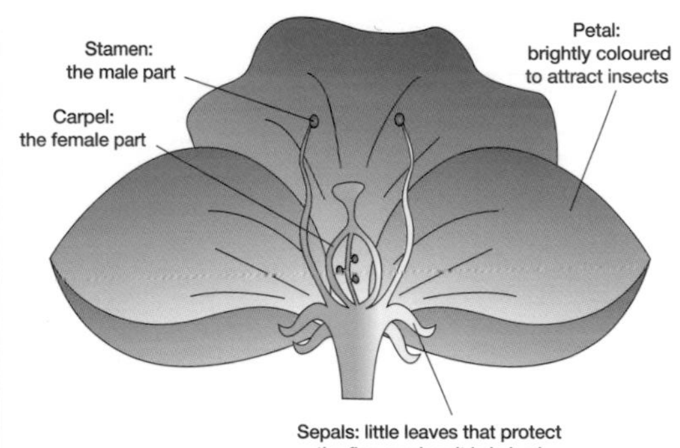

The stamen is the male part of the flower.

The carpel is the female part of the flower, and is made up of the ovary, the stigma and the style.

The Carpel

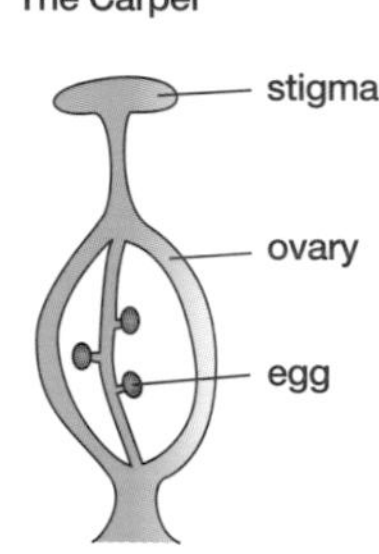

The Stamen

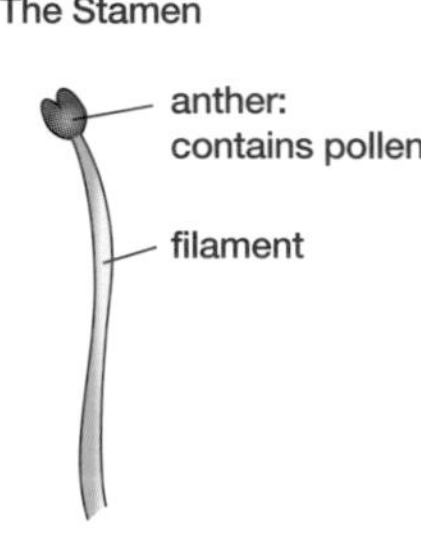

Pollination and Fertilisation

- **A grain of pollen contains a male sex cell.**
- **Grains of pollen get carried to the stigma (female part) by insects or wind. This is called pollination.**
- **The male sex cell travels through a tube down to the ovary, where it meets up with an egg.**
- **The male sex cell and the female egg join together. This is fertilisation.**
- **The fertilised egg grows into a seed.**

Parent's Guide

The test may ask children to label parts of a flower and describe the processes of pollination and fertilisation. They need to understand the life-cycles of plants and how seeds can be distributed.

Seeds and Fruits

Seeds are the fertilised eggs of plants. If circumstances are right, they will be able to grow into new plants.

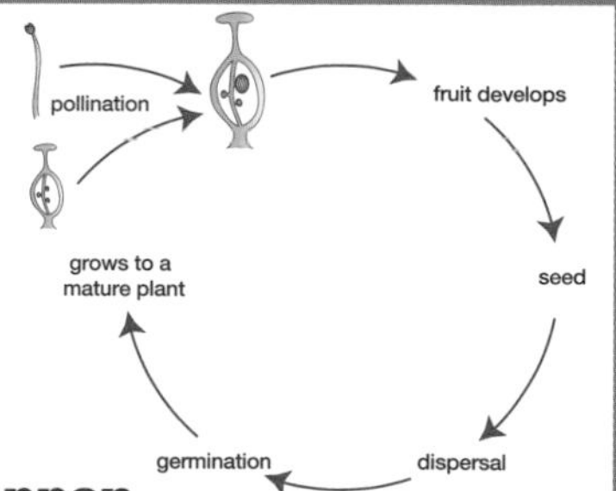

Life Cycle of Plants

Before the seed can begin to grow, several things have to happen.

- **The flower dies while the ovary, the female part that contained the eggs, develops into a fruit.**
- **The seeds need to be dispersed; they need to travel away from the parent plant, otherwise there would be overcrowding.**

Questions

1. What does germination mean?
2. Which part of a flower grows into the fruit?
3. Name three methods of seed dispersal.

Activity

Buy some strawberries or raspberries. Look at them carefully and you will see that the seeds grow on the outside of the berry. Can you find the seeds in bananas and apples?

Seed Dispersal

Seeds can be dispersed in a number of ways:

By animals
Animals eat tasty fruits and the seeds drop to the ground in their waste, e.g. apples, cherries, nuts and berries. Seeds of some plants are sticky or have little 'hooks' so they get trapped in animal fur.

By the wind
The wind carries lightweight seeds away from the parent plant, e.g. dandelion and grass seeds.

By explosion
Seed pods (the fruit skin) pop open and seeds fly out, e.g. peas.

Germination

When the seed falls to the ground, it will only grow if it has water, air and warmth. A seed that is beginning to grow is germinating. Seeds contain a store of food so they do not need to photosynthesise. This means that seeds can grow in the dark – in the soil.

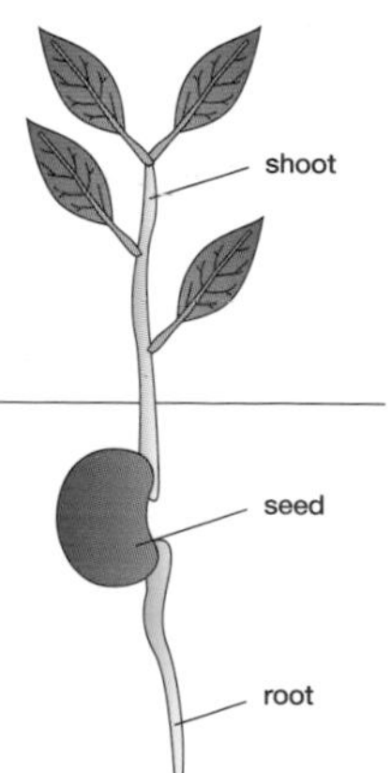

Classification

Scientists find it easier to sort out animals and plants if they put them into groups. This is called classification.

Did You Know?

There are at least 250,000 species, or different types, of beetle in the world?

- **Animals and plants are classified into different groups.**
- **Similar animals or plants are put into the same group.**
- **Similar animals or plants share characteristics, e.g. having a shell.**

These are groups of similar animals: some are cat-like, some are dog-like.

Cat-like animals:
Leopard
Lion
Cheetah
Siamese cat
Puma
Cougar
Jaguar
Tiger

Dog-like animals:
Red Fox
Arctic Fox
Wolf
Alsatian
Dingo
Jackal
Wild dog
Coyote

Here are some characteristics you might use to classify animals:

Feathers
Fur
Hoofed feet
Slimy skin
Breathe using gills
Can fly

Can you think of any others?

Questions

Make three groups according to these animals' characteristics. Which characteristics did you use?

salmon	cow	snail
goat	worm	trout
camel	ant	cod

Activity

Make up your own list like the one above and ask someone else to create groups from it. Do you agree with the characteristics they chose?

Parent's Guide

The National Curriculum suggests that children use the subject of classification as an opportunity to practise their computer skills. They could create a branching database on a computer and develop keys for classification.

The Classification of Animals

Animals can be divided into two, very large groups.

Invertebrates	Vertebrates
Animals without a backbone, e.g. slugs, snails, insects, beetles, octopuses, jellyfish, worms	**Animals with a backbone. This group can be divided into five main groups:**

Fish

Live in water, breathe using gills.
Have fins, lay eggs in water.
e.g. goldfish, sharks.

Amphibians

Breathe through gills when young, then with lungs.
Lay eggs in water.
e.g. frogs and toads.

Reptiles

Breathe with lungs.
Have scaly skin.
Lay eggs on land.
e.g. snakes, lizards and crocodiles.

Birds

Breathe with lungs.
Have feathers.
Lay eggs on land.
e.g. sparrow, emu.

Mammals

Breathe with lungs
Give birth to live young.
Have fur or hair.
e.g. mice, whales.

Questions

Put these animals in the right groups:

1. Python

2. Great White Shark

3. Humans

Activity

Research five animals on the Internet or in the library. See if you can discover anything about their classification. All organisms are given Latin names. Can you think of a good reason for this?

Food Chains and Habitat

Food Chains

Green plants take the raw materials of Sun, water and carbon dioxide to produce food.

- **Green plants are called producers.**
- **Animals eat plants – they are called consumers.**
- **Predators are consumers that hunt for their food, e.g. lions.**
- **Nearly all food chains begin with a green plant producer.**

Remember

Consume means 'to eat'.
Produce means 'to make'.
Predate means 'to hunt'.

Food chains show the relationship between producers and consumers. They help us to understand how plants and animals depend upon one another.

These simple food chains show how food passes from the producer to consumers.

grass producer	→	**cow** consumer	→	**humans** consumer
grass producer	→	**zebra** consumer	→	**lioness** consumer predator

Questions

1. What is a consumer?

2. What is a predator?

Activity

Draw two food chains. One should include a tadpole and the other should include a snail. How are the animals in your food chains adapted to their habitats?

Habitat

The place an animal or plant lives is called its habitat. There are different foods in different habitats and plants and animals are adapted to life in their habitats.

The Arctic Circle is a cold habitat with little vegetation (plants). Polar bears have thick fur to keep them warm and they eat fish and seals.

The jungles are damp, hot habitats, full of plants and trees. Snakes thrive on the bugs and small mammals they can find here.

Parent's Guide

There is a great deal of information available to children about the environment. The library is a good source of books on the topic. For more up-to-date information, check the newspapers regularly or look up conservation web-sites.

Micro-organisms

HEADTEACHER'S AWARD

Tiny organisms that we can't see without a microscope are called micro-organisms. Micro-organisms belong to a separate group from either animals or plants.

Micro-organisms may be very small but they still matter....

There are three main types of micro-organisms. Some are harmful and some are useful.

Questions

1. Name one use of micro-organisms

2. Name one disease caused by viruses.

3. Why should you wash your hands before you eat?

Activity

Look in your fridge and check all the 'use by' dates. Uncooked meat should be kept separate from cooked meat. Are all the foodstuffs covered to prevent drips?

Viruses

Viruses are sometimes called 'germs'.

Some viruses are responsible for making people, plants and animals ill. Measles, chicken pox and the common cold are all caused by viruses. Medicines are not usually good at killing viruses – that's why doctors can not cure a cold.

Bacteria

Bacteria are also sometimes called 'germs'.

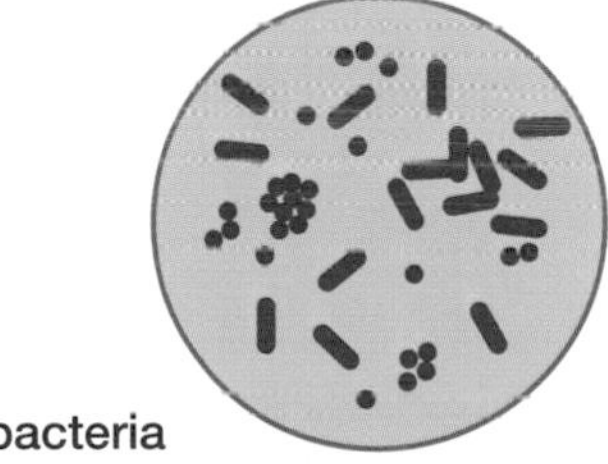
bacteria

We could not live without bacteria; we have useful types in our guts that help us to digest our food. Bacteria help to break down, or rot, dead things. Imagine if nothing dead ever rotted away! Some bacteria cause disease or illnesses, such as food poisoning. That's why it is important to cover food and keep kitchens clean.

Fungi

Mushrooms are fungi – but because they are large they are not micro-organisms.

Tiny fungi can spread in the air and cause mould to grow on food. Mouldy food can make you ill. Fungi, like bacteria, can be useful in causing rot, or decay, of dead things. Yeast is a type of fungi that is used to make bread and beer.

Materials

The word 'material' describes what things are made from. There are many types of material.

Many things are made of a mixture of materials. Look at your shoes – what materials were used to make them?

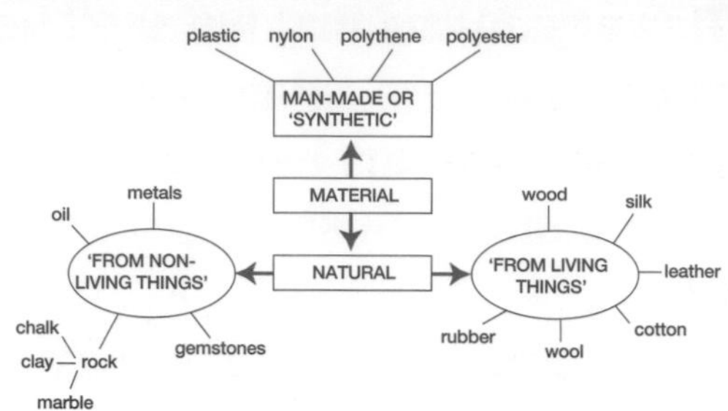

Properties of Materials

Materials have properties that make them useful for certain jobs.

Examples:

Hard Shiny Conducts electricity
Magnetic Strong Flexible (bendy)
Waterproof Absorbent Transparent

Questions

1. Where do metals come from?

2. Why is mercury an unusual metal?

Activity

Find out what material glass is made from. You might be surprised! What properties of glass make it useful? Does it have some properties that are not so good?

States of Materials

A material's state can be solid, liquid or gas.

Materials are made up of lots of tiny, invisible particles. How these particles are arranged determines their state.

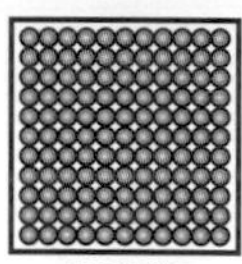
SOLID

A solid does not change its shape when moved and cannot be squashed, e.g. wood, metal.

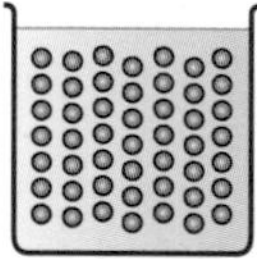
LIQUID

A liquid flows and takes the shape of its container, e.g. oil, water. Mercury is a metal with a liquid state.

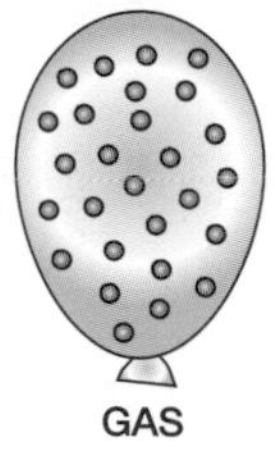
GAS

Gases are usually invisible and spread out to fill up spaces, e.g. air is a mixture of gases including oxygen.

Parent's Guide

The National Curriculum states that children should be able to describe rocks and soils on the basis of their characteristics. Help your child to do this by pointing out different rocks and soils to them. Talk about their properties.

Conductors and Insulators

We've been looking at the properties of materials. Conduction and insulation are very important properties.

Questions

Are the following statements true or false?

1. A good insulator is a poor conductor.

2. Water conducts electricity.

3. Trapped air in duvets helps them insulate heat.

HEADTEACHER'S AWARD

Activity

In your kitchen find three things that conduct heat and three that insulate it.

Conducting Heat

- **A material that conducts heat is one that allows heat to pass through it quickly.**
- **A material that conducts heat is known as a thermal conductor.**
- **Thermal conductors are often metals.**

Insulating Heat

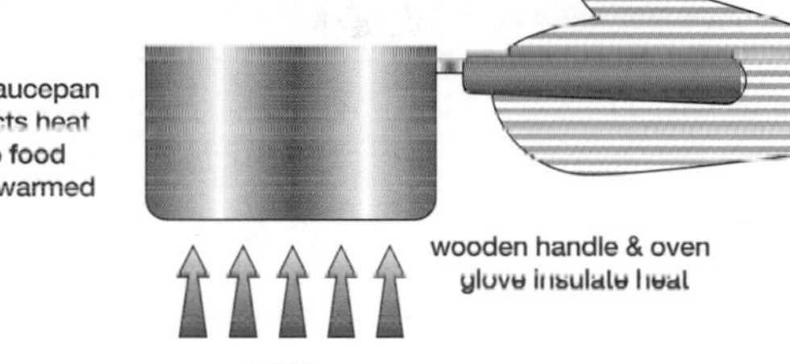
Metal saucepan conducts heat so the food may be warmed
wooden handle & oven glove insulate heat
HEAT

- **A material that insulates heat is one that only allows heat to pass through it slowly.**
- **A material that insulates heat is known as a thermal insulator.**
- **Thermal conductors include materials such as wood, plastic and wool.**

Conducting Electricity

- **A material that conducts electricity is one that lets electricity through.**
- **A material that conducts electricity is called an electrical conductor.**
- **Electrical conductors include metals, salty water and pencil lead (graphite).**

Insulating Electricity

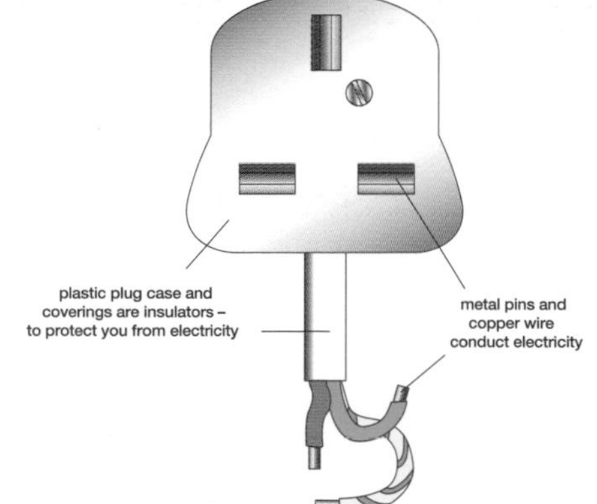
plastic plug case and coverings are insulators – to protect you from electricity
metal pins and copper wire conduct electricity

- **A material that insulates electricity is one that prevents the flow of electricity.**
- **A material that insulates electricity is called an electrical insulator.**
- **Electrical insulators include wood, glass and rubber.**

Effect of Temperature

We can change materials by heating them or freezing them. Sometimes we can change them back again, sometimes we can't.

- **Some changes are reversible – we can change them back.**
- **Some changes are irreversible – we cannot change them back.**

Melting chocolate → reversible change
Frying an egg → irreversible change

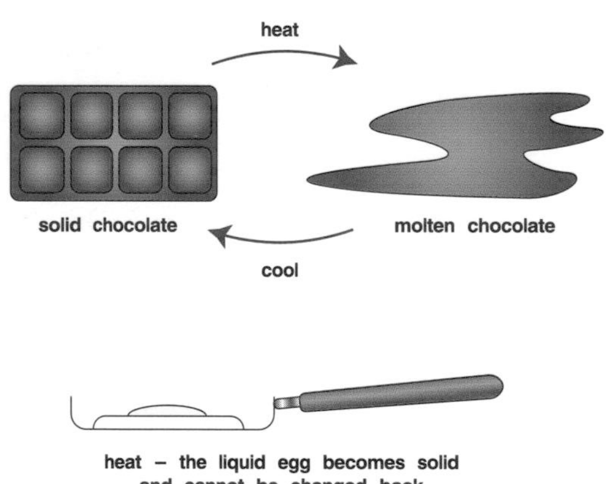

Questions

These changes are reversible, true or false?

1. Dough to bread.

2. Melting butter.

3. Burning coal.

Activity

Take a bath or shower then look at the bathroom window. Can you describe how the droplets of water (condensation) got to be there?

When a material changes

- **from solid to liquid, we say it has melted.**
- **from liquid to gas, we say it has evaporated.**
- **from a gas back to a liquid, after being cooled, we say it has condensed.**

Sometimes heat causes a material to burn. This is an irreversible change but it can produce heat energy, which we use, e.g. burning of oil, gas and coal.

Changes to Water

Water can change states from solid to liquid to gas depending on the temperature. These are reversible changes and mean that water on Earth is constantly being recycled.

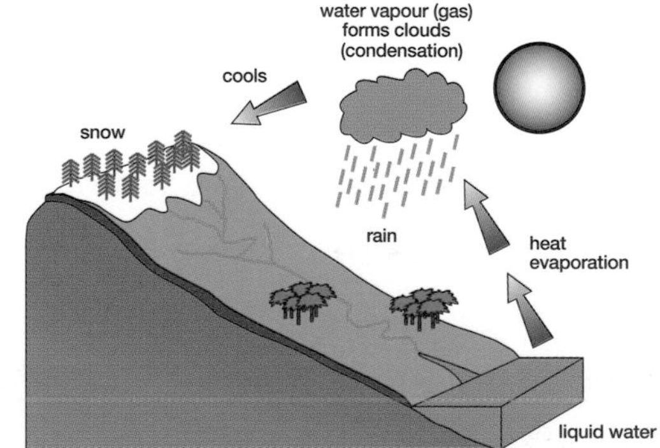

This illustration shows the water cycle.

Parent's Guide

This topic provides an ideal opportunity to do some practical experimenting in the kitchen. Raid the fridge and ask your children what will happen to various materials if you heat or freeze them. Test those predictions and help your child record the results in a table.

Changing Materials

HEADTEACHER'S AWARD

Mixing Materials

You can sometimes mix solids together to produce a new material, e.g. sand, stone and cement, mixed together, produce concrete.

You can mix solids and liquids too, e.g. mix banana (a solid) and toffee sauce (a liquid).

You can mix two liquids, e.g. add milk to a mug of tea, and stir.

Questions

1. What is a solution?

2. Name three soluble solids.

3. Adding bubble bath to bathwater under a running tap is mixing liquids and a gas. What effect does the gas have on the water?

Activity

Using a measuring jug and scales, measure 250 ml of water and 10 g of salt into a bowl and stir. What happens to the salt?

You can mix liquid and a gas, e.g. beat air into an egg and you can make meringue.

Do you think any of these changes are reversible?

Dissolving Solids in Water

Some solids can be mixed with water. If they disappear into the water they are said to have dissolved.

- When a solid dissolves in water a solution has been created.
- Solids that dissolve in water are said to be soluble.
- Solids that do not dissolve in water are said to be insoluble.
- Solids dissolve better in heated water, and when they are stirred.

Soluble solids include salt, aspirin, sugar and instant coffee.

the solid mixes with the water to make a clear solution

Insoluble solids include sand, chalk and flour and ground coffee.

the water may look cloudy and no matter how much you stir, the solid is still there

Sieving and Filtering

We know that we can mix some materials and that the change is irreversible. However, we can mix some materials and then separate them again. There are two ways to do this: sieving and filtering.

Questions

How would you separate:

1. A mixture of granulated sugar and sugar cubes?

2. A mixture of soil and water?

Activity

There are other ways of separating mixtures. Pour some water and oil into a jug and stir. When they have settled see if you can find a way to remove some of the oil. Get an adult to help you.

Sieving

A sieve can be used to separate a mixture of a solid and a liquid, as long as the solid particles are bigger than the holes.

EXAMPLE:
A colander is a type of sieve used in the kitchen to strain vegetables from their cooking water.

A sieve can separate a mixture of solids of different sizes.

EXAMPLE:
Passing flour through a sieve allows the small grains through, but keeps the lumps separate.

Filtering

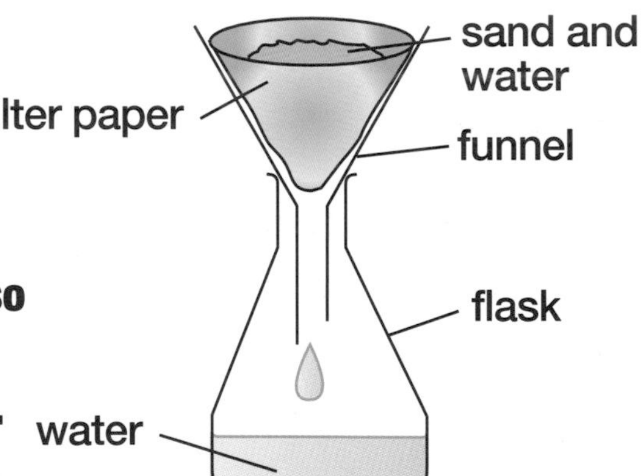

A filter is most often used to separate insoluble solids and liquids. The holes are tiny in a filter, so they can catch even the smallest particles of a solid. This process is called filtration or filtering.

Filter paper, or several layers of kitchen paper, can be used to separate sand from water, which passes through the tiny holes.

Parent's Guide

This topic is closely related to the subjects of materials' properties and states (pages 24–27). The National Curriculum requires children to use their knowledge of liquids, gases and solids to predict how mixtures might be separated. Ensure your child is comfortable with the vocabulary of this topic.

Evaporation

We have seen that insoluble solids may be separated from water by filtration. Soluble solids (ones that dissolve in water) cannot be separated this way; the tiny particles of solid pass right through the filter with the water. But soluble solids may be separated from water by evaporation.

When water is heated it changes from a liquid to a gas. This is evaporation (see page 26).

As the water evaporates, the solid is left behind.

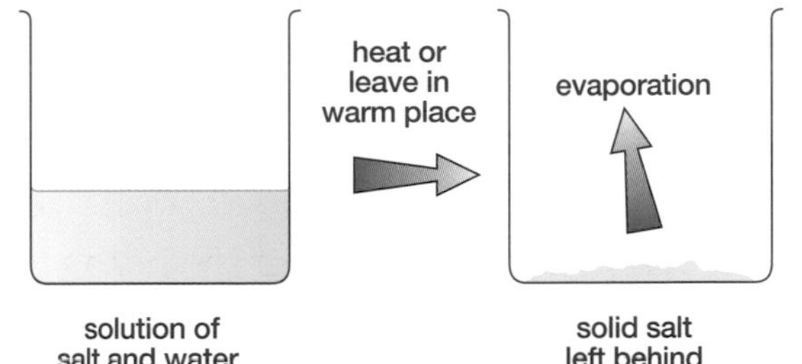

Experiment to Separate Tea Flavour from Tea Leaves and Water

1. With an adult's help pour hot water into a jug containing a tea bag. You will see that the teabag acts as a filter; it keeps the leaves inside but lets the water and tea flavour through.

2. Remove the teabag and pour the tea into a wide dish and either heat it or allow it to dry out in a warm place.

3. When the water has evaporated you will notice that a brown solid (tea) has been left.

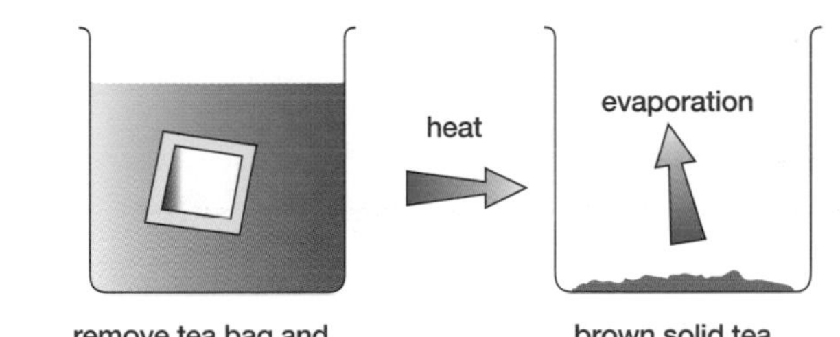

Questions

Give the meanings of these words:

1. Evaporation.

2. Solution.

3. Insoluble.

Activity

Mix sand, salt and water together in a plastic jug. Use filtration and evaporation to separate them. Ask for an adult's permission before you begin, because it could get messy!

Making Simple Circuits

- **We normally get electricity from the mains or batteries.**
- **Mains electricity can be extremely dangerous.**
- **We use batteries to power simple circuits.**
- **A circuit is a complete route or course.**
- **An electrical circuit has electricity flowing through it.**
- **Electricity only flows if the circuit is complete, i.e. there are no gaps.**

An Electrical Circuit

A There is a power source (battery).

C A circuit may contain a component such as a light bulb, buzzer or motor.

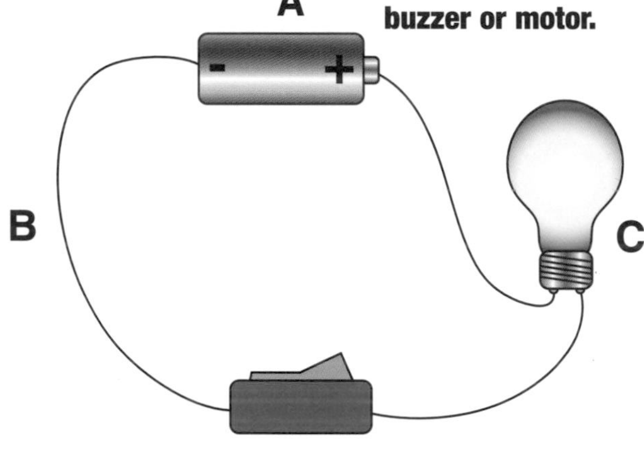

B The electrical wire is a conductor (look at page 25 to remind yourself about conductors and insulators).

D A switch can be used to close or open a circuit. (open = gap, so electricity cannot flow).

Questions

1. Why is electrical wire covered in plastic?

2. Why don't these bulbs light?

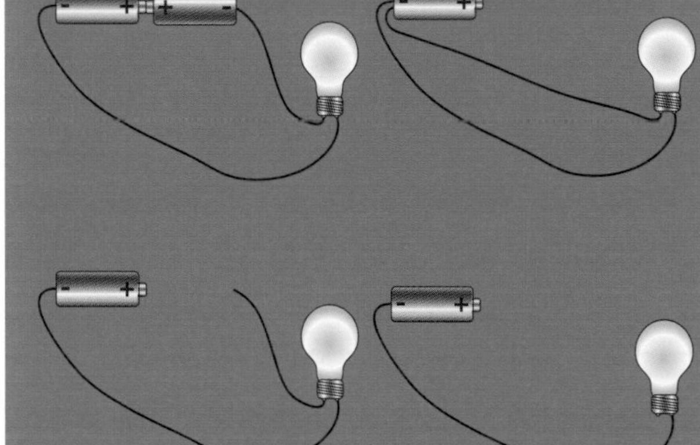

Activity

You must not attempt any electrical experiments at home as they are extremely dangerous. However, you can carry out some simple research. Find out where electricity comes from and how it gets to your house. Use the library or the Internet.

Parent's Guide

Children get the opportunity at school to make electrical circuits, but they may not have had much time to really experiment. Drawing simple circuits helps them to partially overcome this. However, there are things they will just have to learn (see page 31). Ensure their diagrams are clear and accurate.

Drawing Simple Circuits

You must draw your diagrams clearly and accurately.

If necessary, label them – especially if you need to show whether a switch is open or closed.

You must learn what these symbols mean and how to draw them.

Bulb	
Battery	
Two batteries	
Buzzer	
Motor	M
Switch On	
Switch Off	

Questions

Are the following statements true or false?

1. Switches control the flow of electricity.

2. Metal wire is a conductor.

3. This is the symbol for a battery. 

Activity

Draw a number of different circuits then challenge a friend to decide whether they will work or not. See if you can find out what a 'short circuit' is.

You must know that:

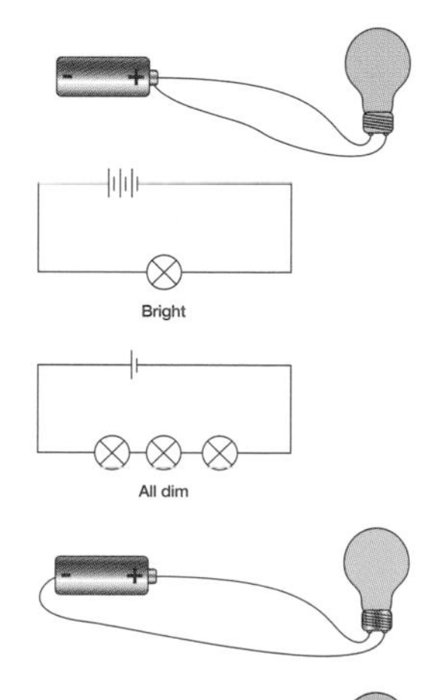

If both ends of the conductor (wire) touch the same end of the battery the circuit will not work.

If you add more batteries in a line, the bulb will be brighter.

If you add more bulbs the light will be fainter in all of them.

The longer the wire, the dimmer the light will be.

A bulb will not work if the conductor is touching the glass of the bulb rather than the metal end.

Forces and Motion

- A force may push or pull something, making it move.
- Forces may make things start, stop, speed up or slow down.
- Forces exist between magnets or between a magnet and certain materials.
- Gravity is a type of force that pulls things towards the centre of the Earth.
- Friction is a type of force that can slow things down.
- Air resistance is a type of friction.
- Forces are measured in Newtons.

Magnets

Magnets have two poles – north and south.

Magnets attract some types of metal, such as iron and nickel. They do not have any effect on non-metals or metals such as copper or gold.

Gravity

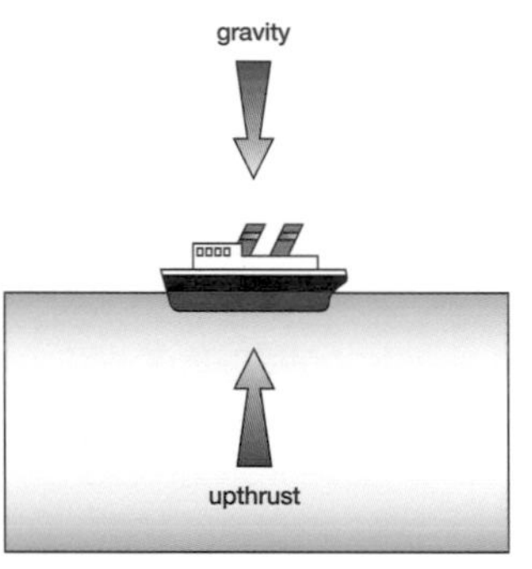

Gravity is the force that keeps us on the planet, rather than spinning into outer space. It is a pulling force, but we can overcome it.

When space rockets take off they overcome gravity to pull upwards by a powerful upthrust from their engines.

When a boat floats on the sea gravity tries to pull it downwards. The water, however, has its own force, or upthrust, which pushes the boat up – keeping it afloat.

Remember

Like poles repel, unlike poles attract. This means that if two magnets are placed next to each other with their north poles almost touching, they will have a force that pushes them apart. If a north pole is placed next to a south pole they will have a force that pulls them together.

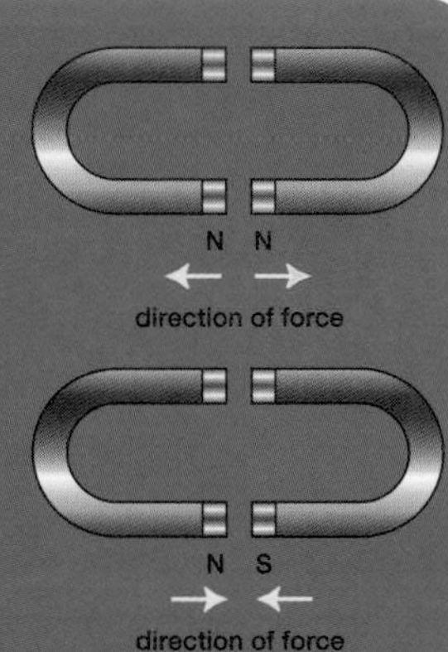

Questions

1. What are the two ways in which forces work?

2. A magnet is placed next to a gold ring. What effect will the magnet have on the ring?

Activity

Use the Internet or the library to discover who Sir Isaac Newton was and why forces are measured in his name.

Parent's Guide

This topic is a very practical one – children can see forces in action all around them. Discuss with your child the way that vehicles may be shaped to reduce air or water resistance. Ask them to think of other ways that friction helps us, or makes life more difficult.

Friction

When two objects rub against each other there is a force between them. This is called friction. Friction slows things down.

EXAMPLE:
Look at these slides. One is covered with sand and the other is covered with water. Which one will be faster to slide down?

The sand will be rough: rough surfaces increase friction and slow things down. The water, however, acts as a lubricant and reduces friction. If you were to slide down the water slide you would zoom right off the end, at great speed!

Questions

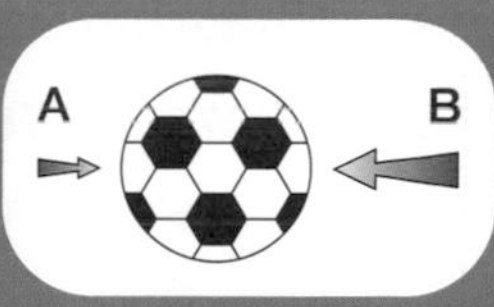

1. This football has a mass of 300 g. It is pulled with a force of ...... newtons.

1. Look at the arrows. Will the ball move towards A or B?

2. Are the forces balanced or unbalanced?

Activity

Draw some diagrams showing 'force arrows' like the ones on this page. Make sure your arrows indicate the direction and strength of a force.

Remember

Air resistance is a type of friction that slows down objects that are moving through air.

When friction is very great, objects may not move at all. Try riding your bike through sand and you will see this for yourself.

Balanced Forces

Every force acts in a particular direction.

When two forces are balanced, things do not start to move.

EXAMPLE:
The size of a force is measured in Newtons. Every 100 g of mass (amount of material) is pulled with a force of 1 Newton. The direction of a force is shown with an arrow. The size of arrow shows the size of the force.

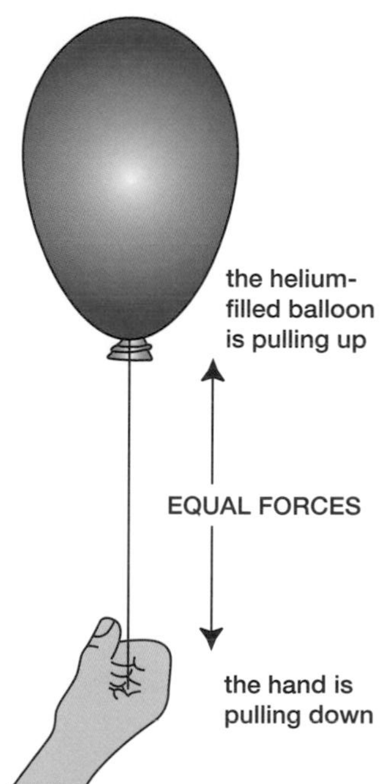

Properties of Light

- Light travels in straight lines.
- Light comes from a light source.

Examples of light sources:

The Sun **Light bulbs** **Candles** **Fire**

Light is reflected off objects and into our eyes – this is how we can see them.

Some objects reflect light better than others and may appear to be sources of light, even though they are not.

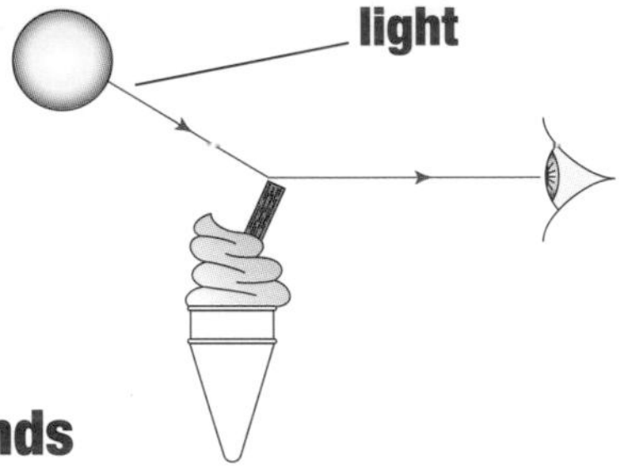

Examples of objects that reflect light:

The Moon **Mirrors** **Metal surfaces** **Diamonds**

Questions

1. The Moon is a light source. True or false?

2. 'Opaque' means see-through. True or false?

Activity

Rest a torch on a book. Put a glass of water 15 cm in front of the torch beam. Place a plain piece of white paper behind the glass and observe the shadow that has been cast. Move the glass either towards the light source or away from it. What do you notice happening to the shadow?

Tip

Transparent: light can travel through transparent objects, e.g. glass and some plastics.
Opaque: light cannot travel through opaque objects, e.g. metal and wood.

Shadows

Light cannot travel through opaque objects; it gets blocked, causing a shadow.

Parent's Guide

Children who find the concepts of light and sound interesting may like to investigate their properties further. Help your child research how light is made up of the colours of the rainbow and how sound travels in waves. The Internet and library can supply the information you need.

Properties of Sound

- **Sound is caused by vibration.**
- **The vibration may be visible, e.g. when a drummer hits the cymbals you can see them shake.**
- **The vibration may be invisible, e.g. when you listen to the radio you cannot see anything vibrate.**
- **Vibrating objects make sound. This sound is passed to our ears and this is how we hear.**

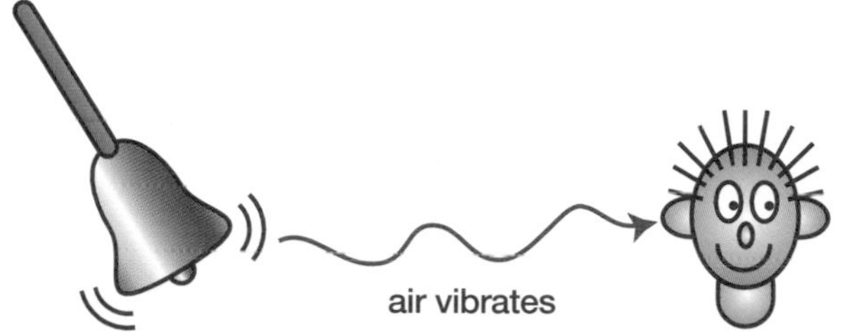

Vibrations may pass through different materials. The vibrations make the air, water or solid materials vibrate too – passing the sound on to our ears.

EXAMPLE:
The sound passes through the wooden table

Volume of Sound

Sounds get louder (Increase in volume) when they vibrate harder. If you are playing the drums, this means you have to beat them harder. If you are playing a wind instrument, such as the oboe, you have to blow a little harder.

Pitch of Sound

Pitch is how high or low a note is. The shorter the vibrating object, the higher the pitch of the note. This is why a violin player moves his or her fingers along the strings, shortening or lengthening them to play different notes.

HEADTEACHER'S AWARD

Questions

1. What does 'pitch' mean?

2. Describe how we hear sound.

3. Sound can travel through water. True or false?

Activity

Experiment with creating different pitches. Line up a series of glass bottles, each containing a different amount of water. Blow across the bottle openings to create sound. Why do you think the fuller bottles produce higher-pitched notes than the emptier ones?

The Earth and Beyond

Our Planet

a half moon is visible – the other half is in the Earth's shadow

light

Moon

Sun

We live on planet Earth – just one of nine planets (that we know about) in our Solar System.

The Sun is the centre of our Solar System and it is our light source.

The Sun, Earth and Moon are all spherical in shape.

The Sun stays where it is: the planets in the Solar System move around it.

The Earth travels all the way around the Sun once every year. This journey is called the Earth's orbit.

The Moon travels around the Earth and it takes 28 days for the Moon to complete its orbit.

The planets stay in their orbits because the Sun's gravity keeps them there.

Remember

Gravity is a type of force that you revised on page 32.

Questions

1. What is an orbit?

2. How many days does it take for the Earth to orbit the Sun?

Activity

Give a grapefruit (the Sun) to one friend, an orange (the Earth) to another and you can hold a grape (the Moon). Now try to recreate the movements of the Sun, Earth and Moon.

The Moon stays in its orbit because the Earth's gravity keeps it there.

As the Moon travels through its orbit, its appearance changes (full Moon, half Moon, crescent Moon).

Parent's Guide

Children are easily confused when trying to visualise the concepts covered on these two pages. Television programmes on astronomy, CD-Roms, videos and activities such as the ones described here can all help a child to imagine how these celestial bodies move, and the effects they have on our seasons.

Day and Night

The Earth spins on its axis once every 24 hours.

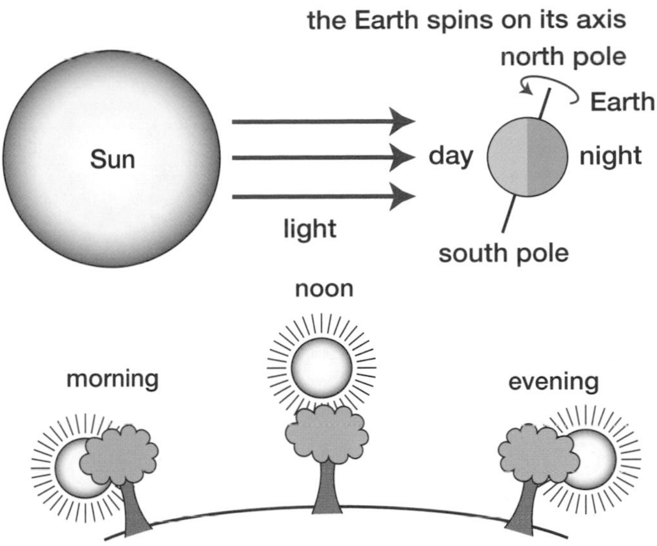

In this picture you can see that the Sun is only shining on one half of the Earth – daytime. The other half of the planet is in darkness – night-time.

As we move from night-time to daytime, the Sun appears to be rising on the horizon. In fact the Sun isn't moving at all – the Earth is.

The Sun rises in the east and sets in the west.

During the morning and evening, shadows are long. At midday shadows are short. Look back at page 34 to remind yourself why this happens.

The Moon does not spin, so one half is in permanent darkness – this is called 'the dark side of the Moon'.

Remember

The Sun rises early in the east and goes to rest in the west.

The Seasons

The Earth is tilted on its axis. This causes different parts of the world to have seasons. When the north of the Earth is tilted towards the Sun, it is summer here. When the north is tilted away from the Sun, we are in our winter.

Questions

1. At what time is the Sun at its highest in the sky?

2. Does the Sun rise in the east or west?

3. Does the Moon have days and nights?

Activity

Use a felt-tip pen to mark the position of the United Kingdom on an orange. In a darkened room shine a torch on the United Kingdom and slowly turn the orange round. This will show you how the rotation of the Earth causes days and nights.

HEADTEACHER'S AWARD

Introduction to Practice Test Papers

The National Tests

Children at the end of Key Stage 2 (Year Six) take tests in English, maths and science. Each subject in the National Curriculum is divided into core subjects. In science, for example, these are:

- Scientific Enquiry
- Life Processes and Living Things
- Materials and their Properties
- Physical Processes

Targets are set for achievement within these core subjects.
In science, for example, 'Physical Processes' includes:

- Electricity
- Forces and Motion
- Light and Sound
- The Earth and Beyond

A combination of written tests, (SATs, or NCTs) and continuous classroom assessment enables the teachers to record the targets individual children have met.

What do SATs Involve?

The children are given written papers to complete. In science they have two or three papers:
Tests A and B are each 35 minutes long and are taken by all children. Both tests are used to assess Levels 3-5 (see below).
Test C is 30 minutes long. It is used to assess children who are working at Level 6. Your child is unlikely to take Test C: it is given to children who are expected to achieve Level 5 easily and are working at an exceptional level in science.

How are National Tests marked?

Children sit the exams in May and the test papers are sent away for marking. Results come back in July.

- Most children will achieve results between Level 3 and Level 5.
- Level 3 indicates that extra work is required to reach the target for this age group.
- Level 4 indicates that targets set for this age group have been attained.
- Level 5 or above indicates that the targets for their age group have been exceeded.
- Generally, children are expected to move up one level every two years.

What are National Test Results Used For?

SATs results may indicate several things:

- Whether a child progressing through the levels appropriately.
- Whether a school is doing well.
- Areas of weakness that a child might need extra help with.
- Test results may also be used, with other assessments, to help Year 7 teachers decide how to allocate children to suitable ability groups or classes.

How Should I Use the Practice Papers?

In this section of the book you will find examples of all three types of test. Your child should not attempt to take any of the tests until they have, at least, skimmed through the revision section and answered the questions they encountered on the way.

It can be de-motivating to do badly in a test. Ensure your child has a good understanding of the concepts and techniques used in each Practice Paper before they attempt it.

Encourage your child to complete a Practice Test paper in real exam conditions. This means no help and no breaks.

Answers are in the back of the book. It is essential that you help your child to correct any mistakes they make. Heap plenty of praise on them for the work they complete correctly and reward them for good corrections that are done promptly.

If your child continues to struggle with a subject you should discuss this with their teacher, who may be able to suggest an alternative way of helping your child.

Test 1
Level 3–5

Instructions

Read this carefully.

Answers

This shows where you will need to put your answer.

For some questions you may need to draw an answer instead of writing one.

You have 35 minutes for this test.

1. Look at this table. It shows some things that have changed.

Are the changes reversible? Tick one box for each change.

Is this change reversible?

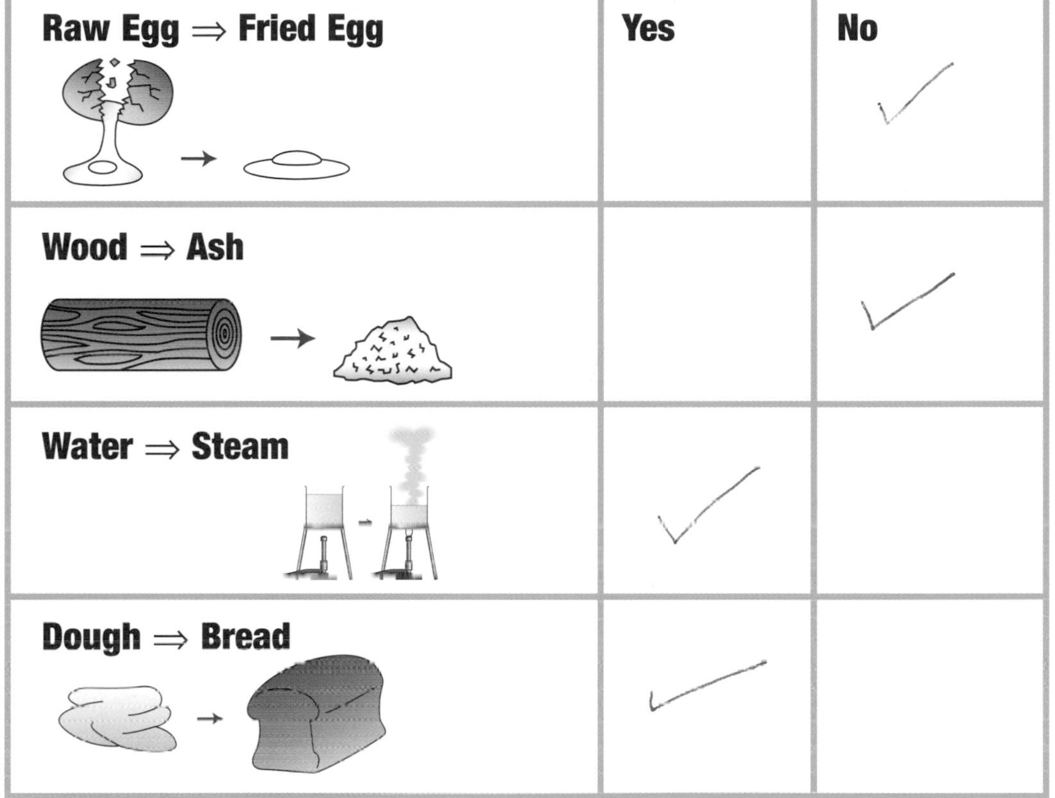

	Yes	No
Raw Egg ⇒ Fried Egg		
Wood ⇒ Ash		
Water ⇒ Steam		
Dough ⇒ Bread		

2. a) Draw three lines to match each of these animals to the environment in which it lives.

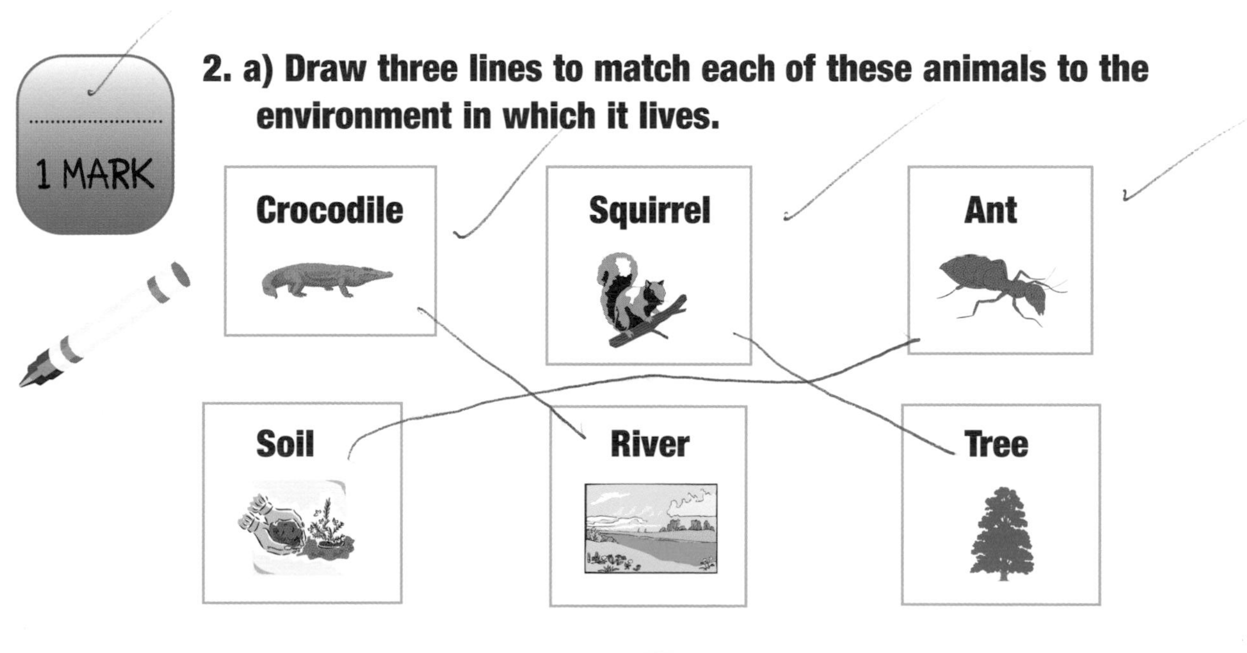

b) These animals live in different environments.

Complete the table below to describe one feature of a camel. Say how the feature helps the camel to live in its environment.

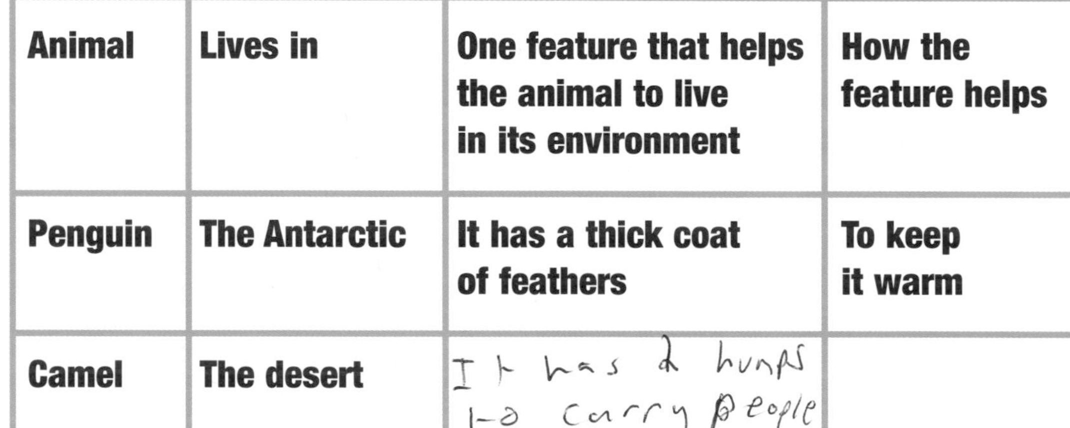

Animal	Lives in	One feature that helps the animal to live in its environment	How the feature helps
Penguin	The Antarctic	It has a thick coat of feathers	To keep it warm
Camel	The desert	It has 2 humps to carry people	

3. Amanda spills some milk, so she mops it up with a paper towel.

a) Why is paper towel a good material to use?

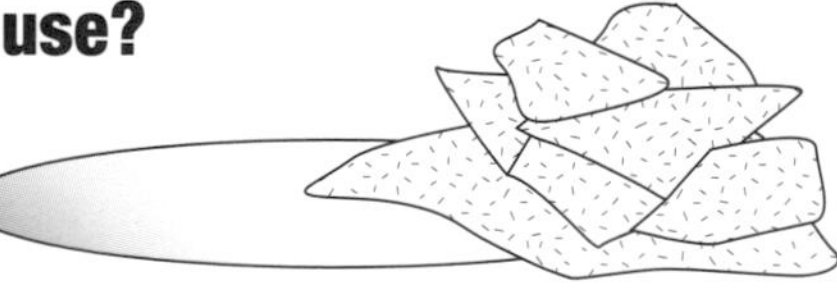

Be cause it obsorbs.

1 MARK

b) Some of the milk has spilt on to the kitchen floor and forms puddles. When Amanda's mum comes home 30 minutes later, the milk puddles are still there.

Tick one box to say why the puddles of milk are still on the floor.

The puddles stay on the floor because the floor tiles

- Are shiny ☑
- Are waterproof ☐
- Are made of a solid material ☐
- Are magnetic ☐

1 MARK

c) Name the process that causes steam to turn into liquid water.

condensation

1 MARK

d) Complete this sequence with these words: ~~liquid~~, ~~solid~~, ~~gas~~.

When I put water in the kettle it is a ...liquid... When it boils it turns into a ...gas... When I put water into the freezer it turns into ice, which is a ...solid...

1 MARK

e) Tick the box that describes the appearance of liquid water.

- Transparent ☑
- Opaque ☐

1 MARK

4. There are Seven Life Processes that all living things share.

a) Match each word to its meaning, by drawing a line. The first one has been done for you.

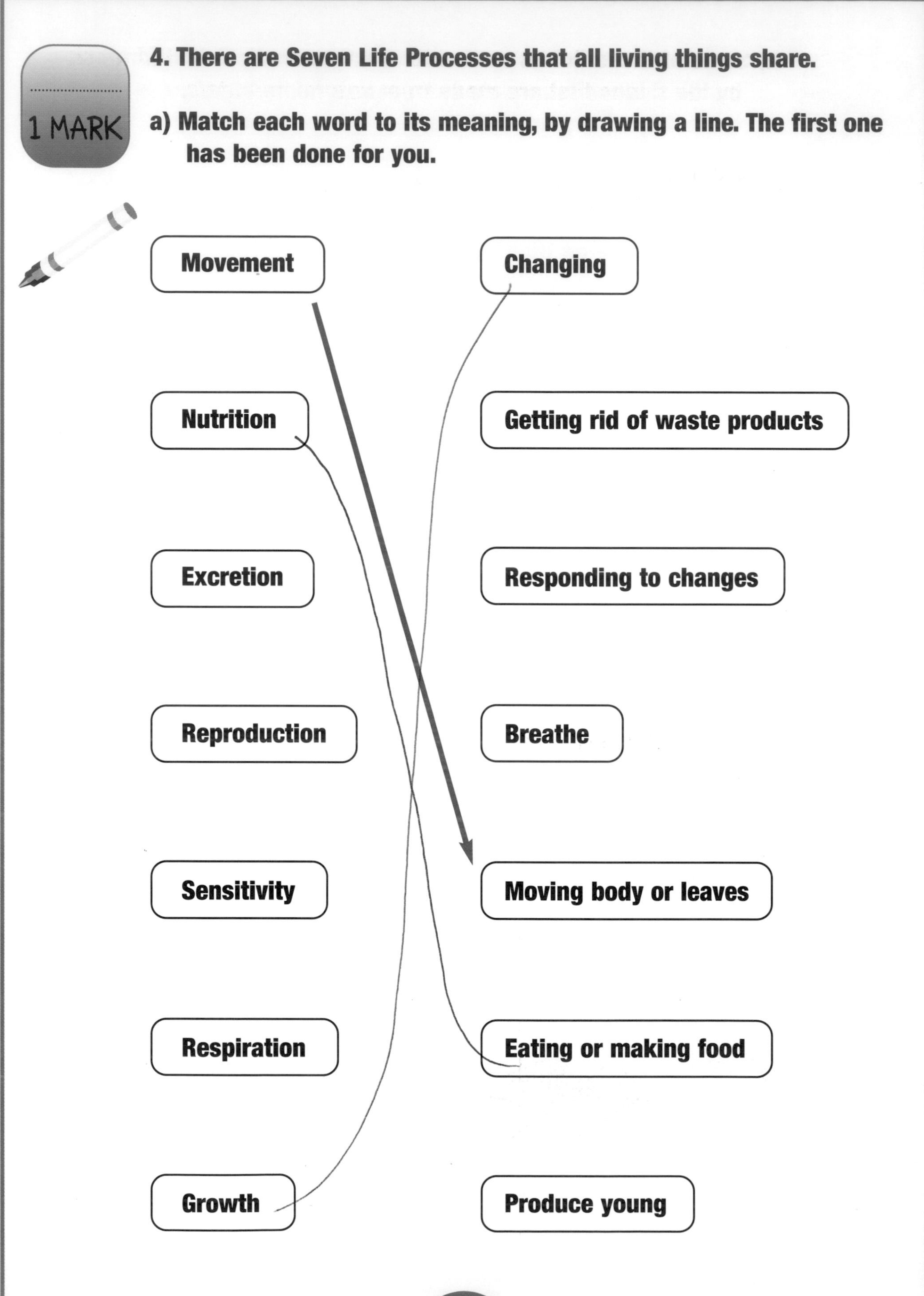

b) Some of these things are made of natural materials. Put a tick by the things that are made from natural materials.

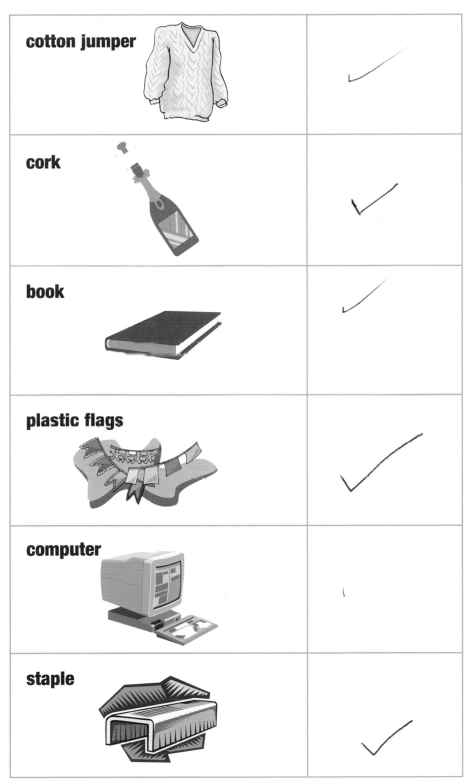

cotton jumper	✓
cork	✓
book	✓
plastic flags	✓
computer	
staple	✓

1 MARK

5. a) Look at the lists below. It shows some materials in one column and some properties in the other. Draw lines to join the materials to their properties. One material has been joined to its property for you.

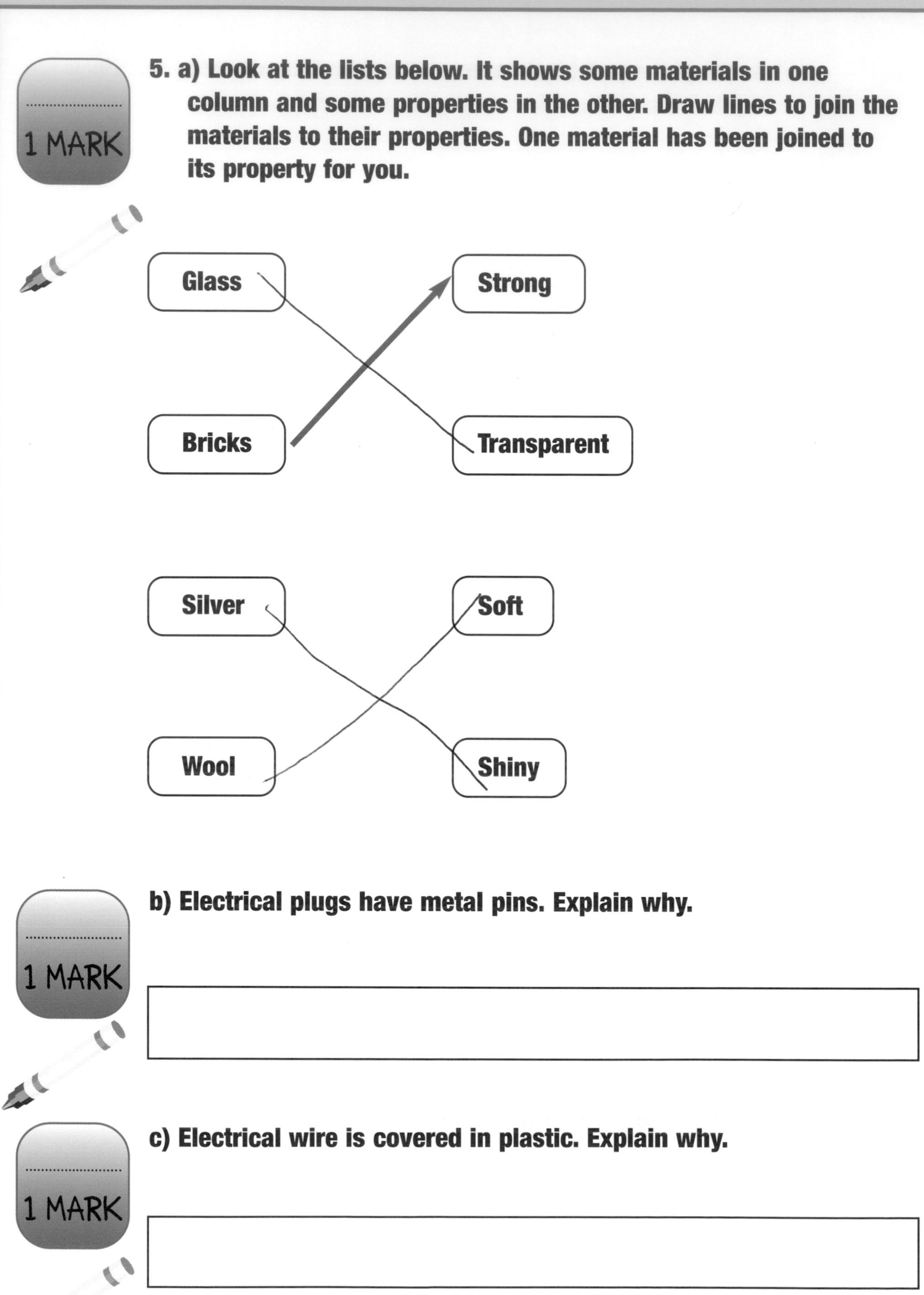

1 MARK

b) Electrical plugs have metal pins. Explain why.

1 MARK

c) Electrical wire is covered in plastic. Explain why.

1 MARK

d) Some of these materials are natural and some are synthetic. Put circles around the synthetic materials.

Plastic

Wood

Polystyrene

Cotton

1 MARK

6. a) Name the parts of the plant

A flower

B stem

C leaf

D root

1 MARK

b) Name three ways in which plants distribute their seeds.

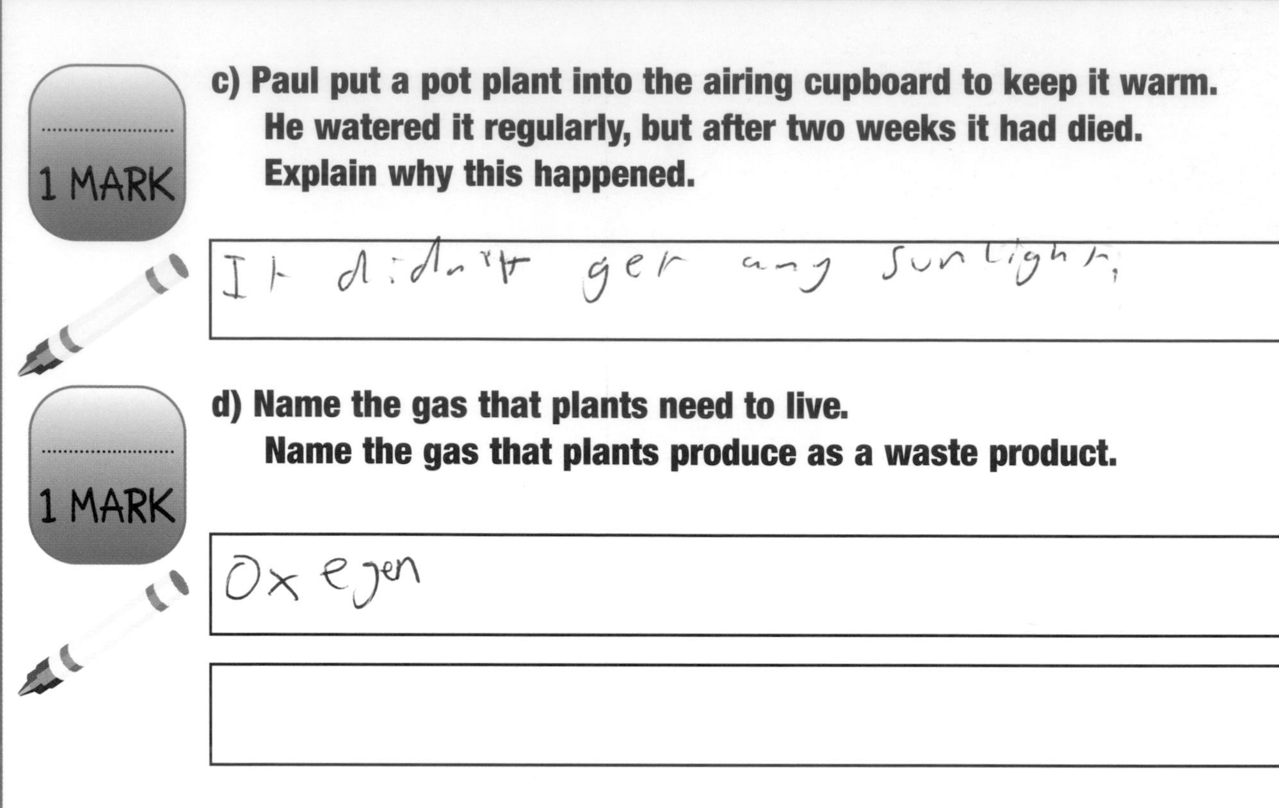

1 MARK
It didn't get any sunlight
1 MARK
Oxejen

c) Paul put a pot plant into the airing cupboard to keep it warm. He watered it regularly, but after two weeks it had died. Explain why this happened.

d) Name the gas that plants need to live. Name the gas that plants produce as a waste product.

7. Natalie is doing a project on the human body. She writes a list to show the functions of different parts of the body.

Functions of parts of the body:

1. Protects the brain
2. Takes in oxygen
3. Supports the body
4. Carries blood around the body
5. Moves the body

1 MARK

a) Which of the functions on Natalie's list is the main function of the muscles?

1 MARK

b) Which of the functions on Natalie's list is the main function of the arteries?

1 MARK

c) Which of the functions on Natalie's list is the main function of the skeleton?

Supports the body.

1 MARK

d) When Natalie presses her finger on her wrist she can feel a beating. Describe what this beating is.

8. a) In each box there are two food or drink choices. Put a tick on the healthier choice in each box.

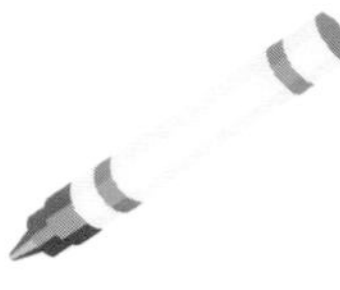

b) Jill has been to the dentist and has had a filling. She does not want to have another one. Suggest three things she should do to keep her teeth healthy in the future.

cut down on sweets
eat 5 and 5E.
drink milk because it strenghtense
the teeth.

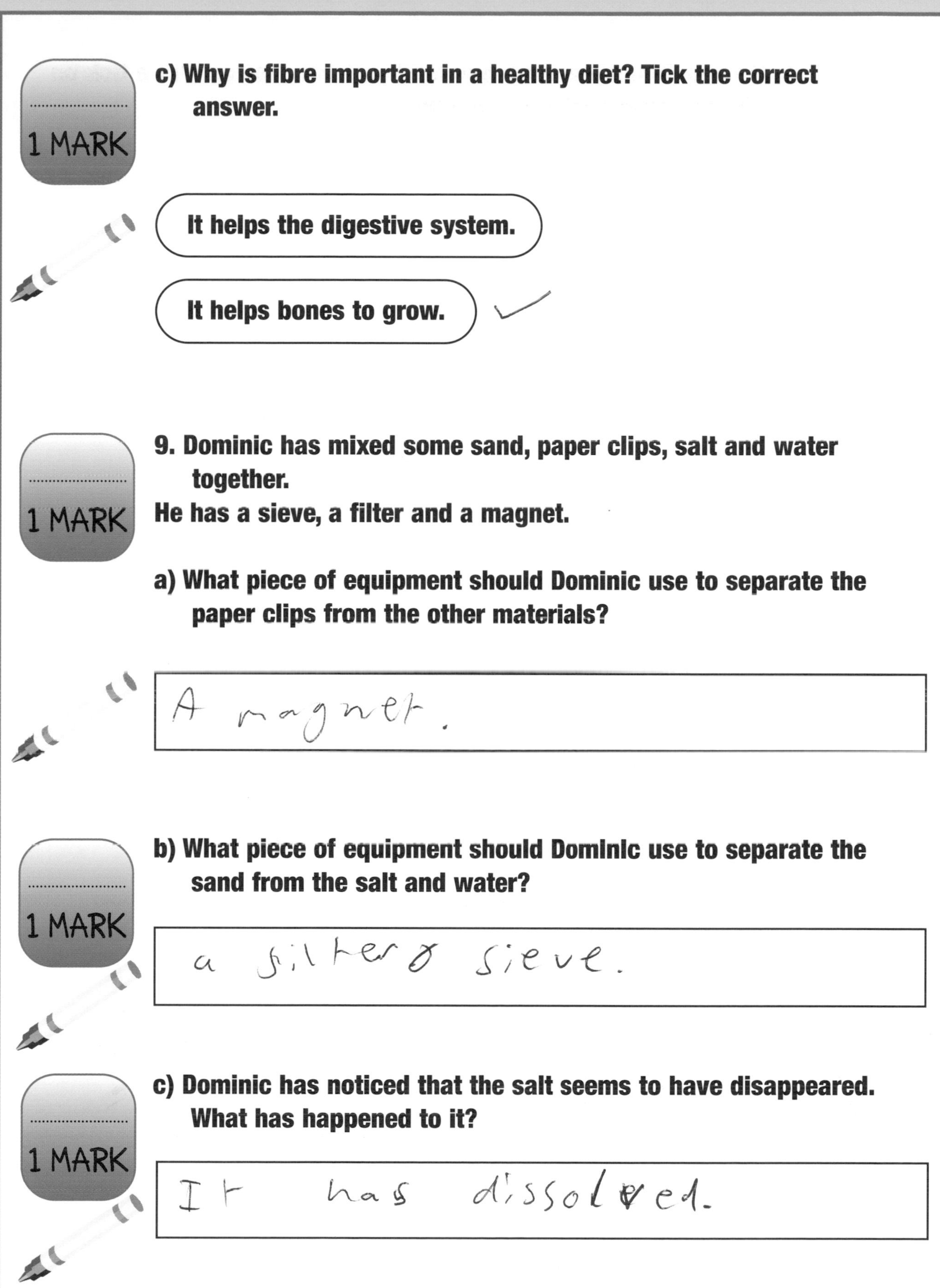

1 MARK

c) Why is fibre important in a healthy diet? Tick the correct answer.

It helps the digestive system.

It helps bones to grow. ✓

1 MARK

9. Dominic has mixed some sand, paper clips, salt and water together.
He has a sieve, a filter and a magnet.

a) What piece of equipment should Dominic use to separate the paper clips from the other materials?

A magnet.

1 MARK

b) What piece of equipment should Dominic use to separate the sand from the salt and water?

a filter ~~or~~ sieve.

1 MARK

c) Dominic has noticed that the salt seems to have disappeared. What has happened to it?

It has dissolved.

1 MARK

d) Dominic manages to separate the salt from the water and ends up with a plate of salt crystals. How did he do this?

1 MARK

10. a) When Linda stands in her garden she notices that her shadow is very short. What time is it? Put a tick in the correct box

Early morning ☐

Midday ☐

Evening ☐

2 MARKS

b) A cloud comes over and Linda's shadow has disappeared. Explain why this happens.

1 MARK

c) After lunch Linda wants to call her cousin in Australia. Her father tells her that it is not a good idea to call Australia at that time.

Why?

Test 2
Level 3–5

Instructions

Read this carefully.

Answers
This shows where you will need to put your answer.

For some questions you may need to draw an answer instead of writing one.

You have 35 minutes for this test.

1 MARK

1. John has seen the following things in his local woods.

John sorts these animals into groups:

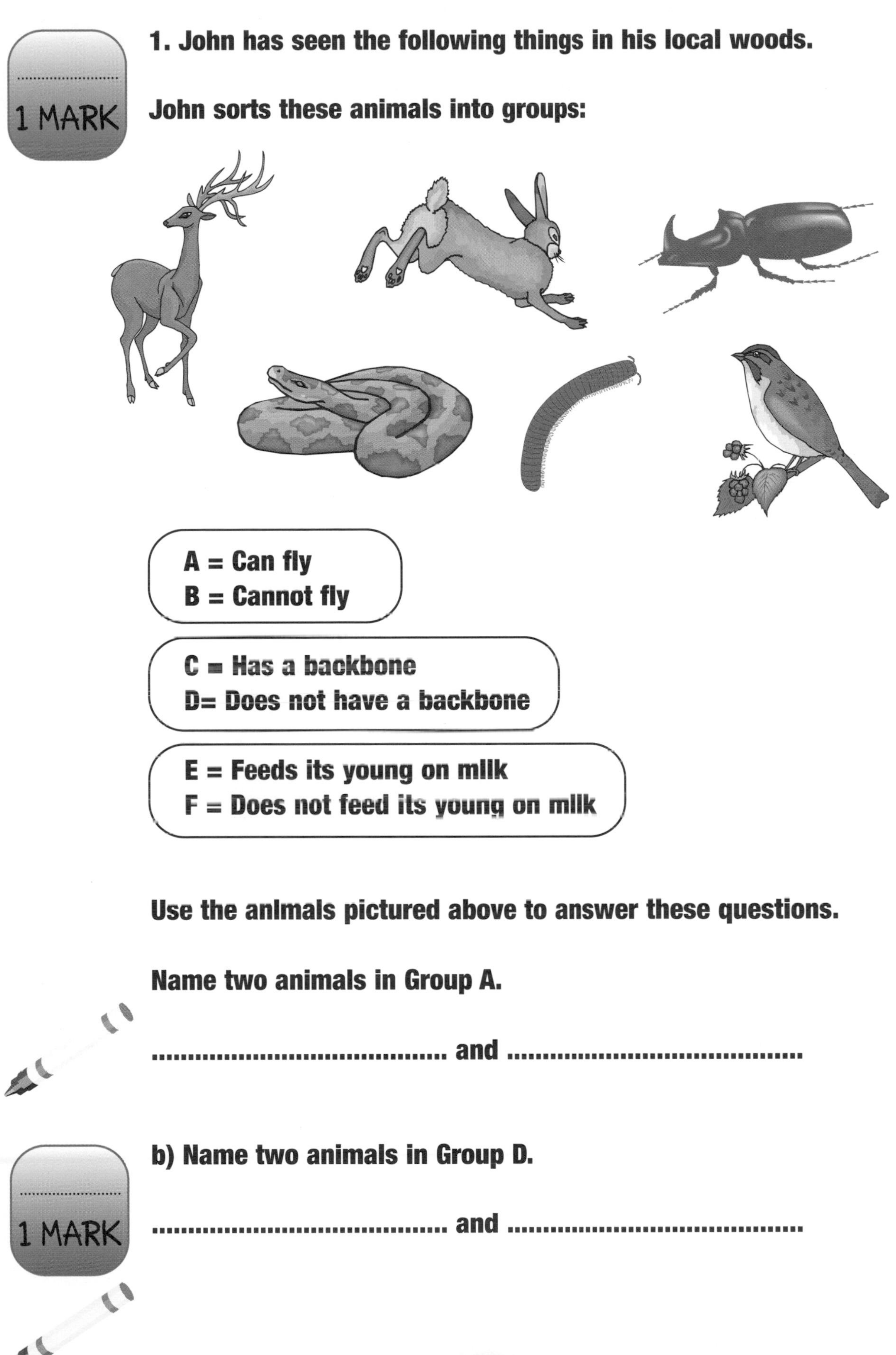

A = Can fly
B = Cannot fly

C = Has a backbone
D= Does not have a backbone

E = Feeds its young on milk
F = Does not feed its young on milk

Use the animals pictured above to answer these questions.

Name two animals in Group A.

.. and ....

1 MARK

b) Name two animals in Group D.

.. and ....

2 MARKS

c) Circle three letters below to show which group an adult human might be in.

A B C D E F

2. a) Look at these pictures.

1 MARK

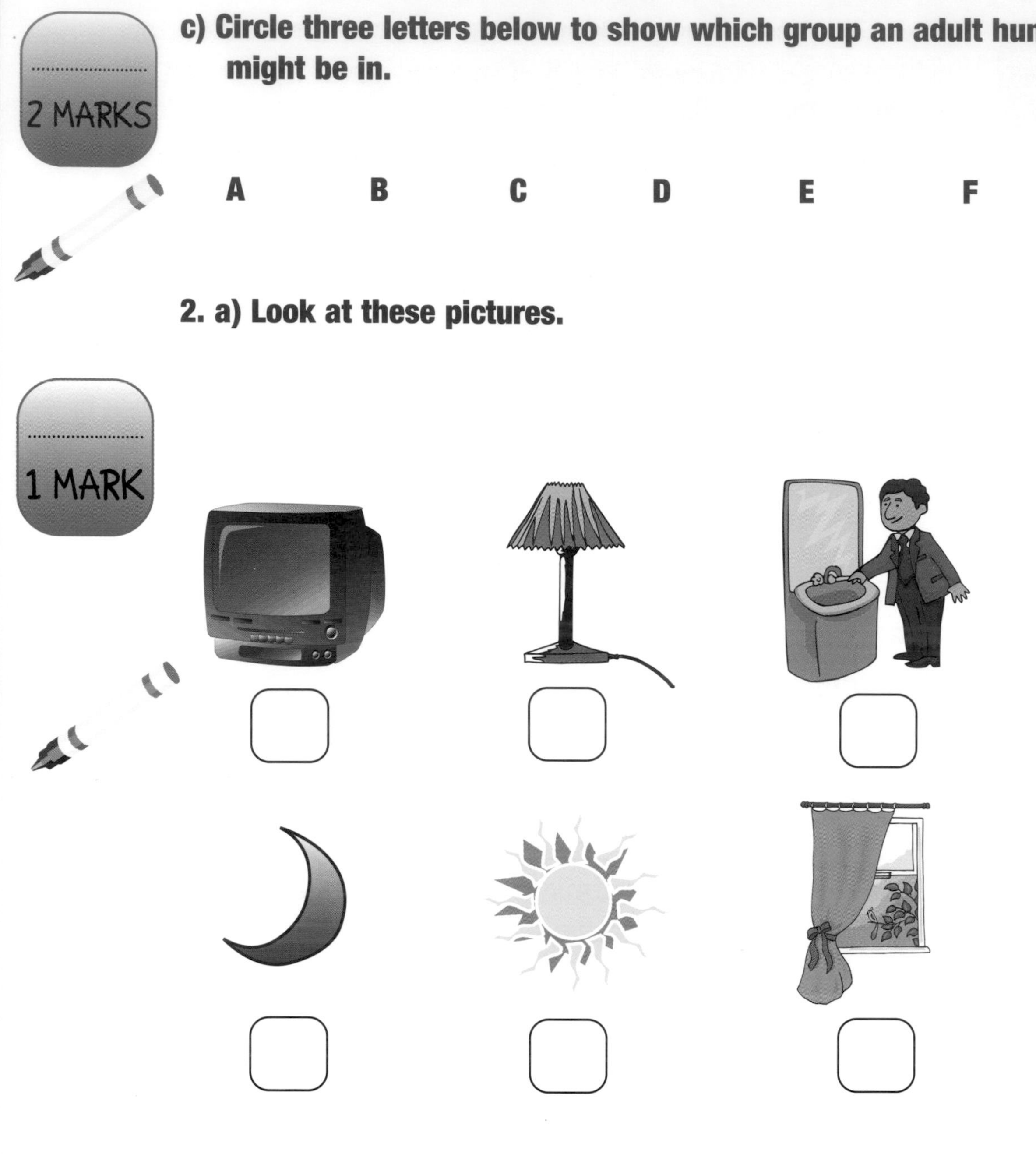

Some of these objects are light sources. Put a tick by the objects that are sources of light.

b) Complete this table to show which of these materials allow light to pass through. The first one has been completed for you.

Material	Some light passes through	No light passes through
Cardboard		✓
Diamond		
Clear plastic		
Tissue paper		
Mirror		

c) Mark sits in a darkened room. He notices that he still has a shadow. Two of these items might be causing the shadow.

Tick the two items that might cast Mark's shadow.

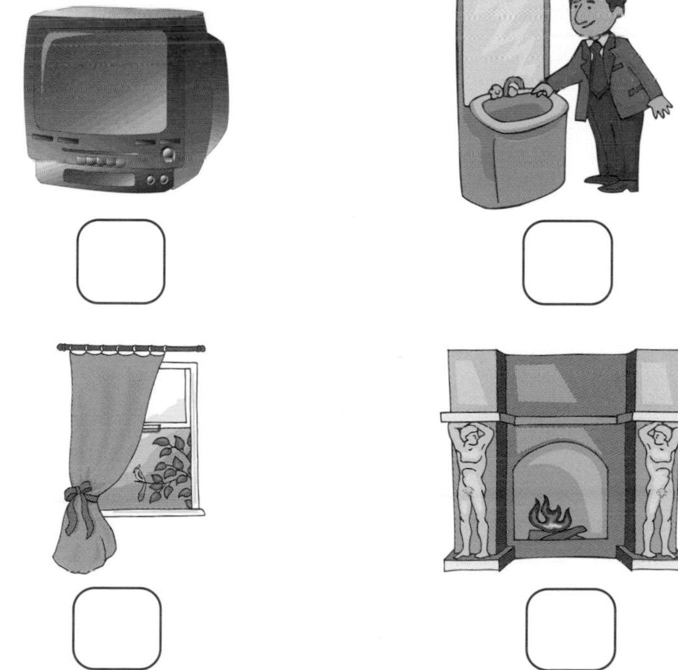

1 MARK

d) Tick one box that explains why these items cast a shadow

They are bright ☐

They are light sources ☐

They are transparent ☐

They let light pass through ☐

1 MARK

3. a) Describe the differences between the two teeth.

A

B

1 MARK

b) Why do you think the teeth look different? Tick the correct box

They belong to different animals ☐

They are found in different parts of the mouth ☐

They have different functions ☐

1 MARK

c) Which tooth would be best for cutting food?

1 MARK

d) Which tooth would be best for grinding food?

1 MARK

4. Marcus is making some jelly. He pours hot water in to a jug then adds the jelly cubes. He watches the change that takes place.

a) Describe what happens to the jelly cubes in the hot water.

1 MARK

b) Is this change reversible?

1 MARK

c) There are still some lumps of jelly at the bottom of the jug. Put a tick by the box that shows what Marcus should do to get all the jelly to mix with the water.

Stir the mixture ☐

Put the mixture into the fridge ☐

Add more jelly cubes ☐

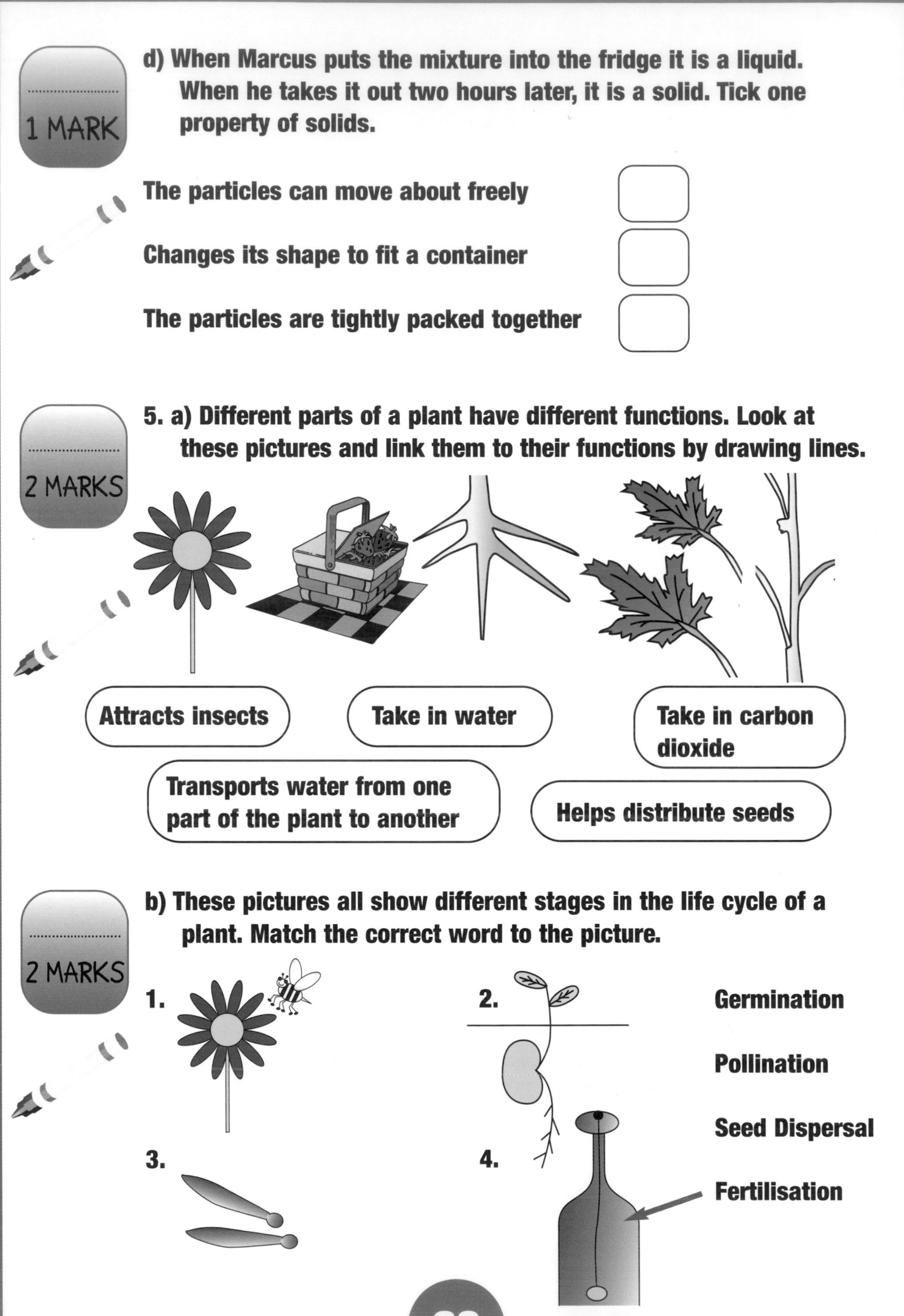

1 MARK

d) When Marcus puts the mixture into the fridge it is a liquid. When he takes it out two hours later, it is a solid. Tick one property of solids.

The particles can move about freely ☐

Changes its shape to fit a container ☐

The particles are tightly packed together ☐

2 MARKS

5. a) Different parts of a plant have different functions. Look at these pictures and link them to their functions by drawing lines.

Attracts insects

Take in water

Take in carbon dioxide

Transports water from one part of the plant to another

Helps distribute seeds

2 MARKS

b) These pictures all show different stages in the life cycle of a plant. Match the correct word to the picture.

1.

2.

3.

4.

Germination

Pollination

Seed Dispersal

Fertilisation

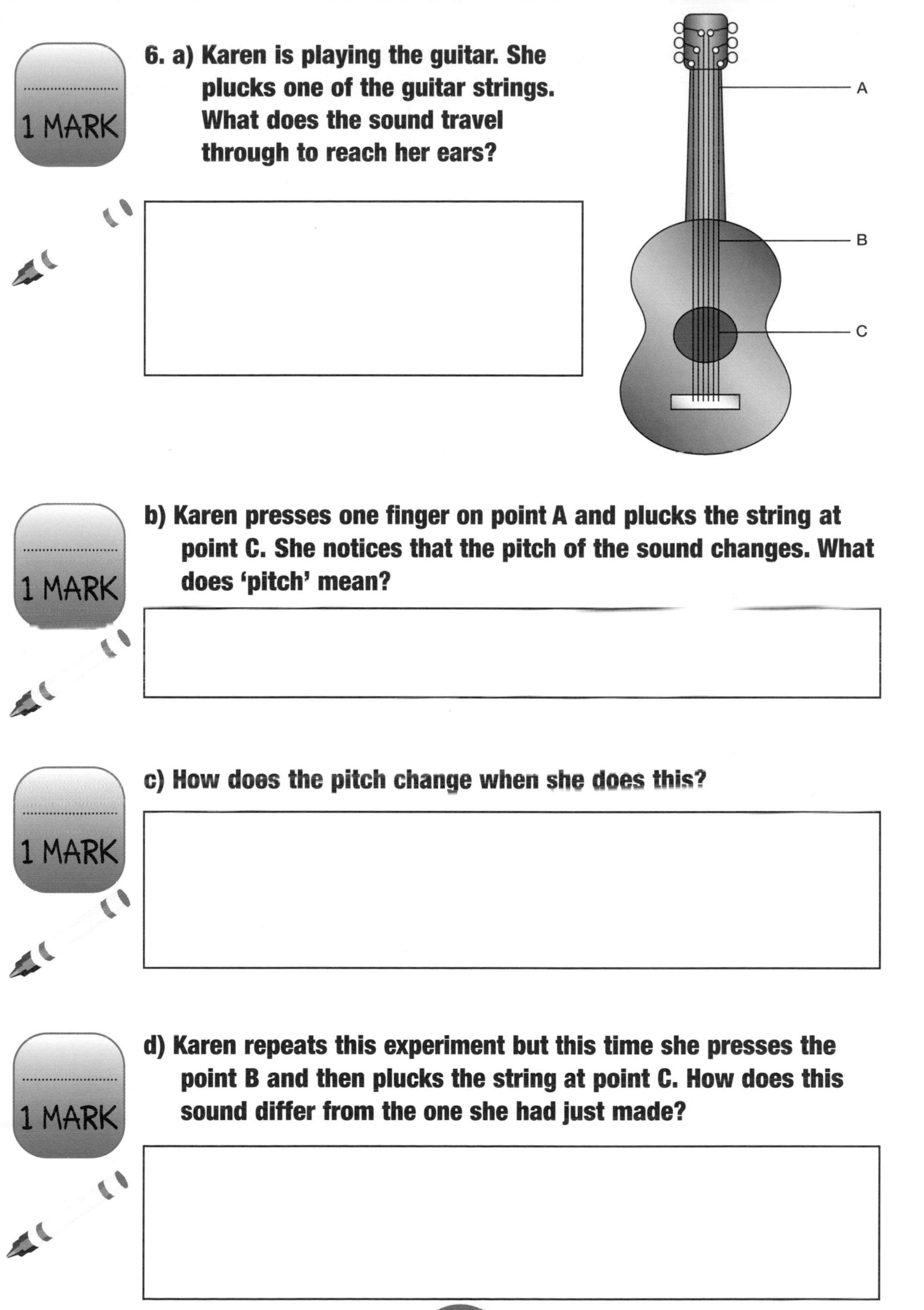

6. a) Karen is playing the guitar. She plucks one of the guitar strings. What does the sound travel through to reach her ears?

b) Karen presses one finger on point A and plucks the string at point C. She notices that the pitch of the sound changes. What does 'pitch' mean?

c) How does the pitch change when she does this?

d) Karen repeats this experiment but this time she presses the point B and then plucks the string at point C. How does this sound differ from the one she had just made?

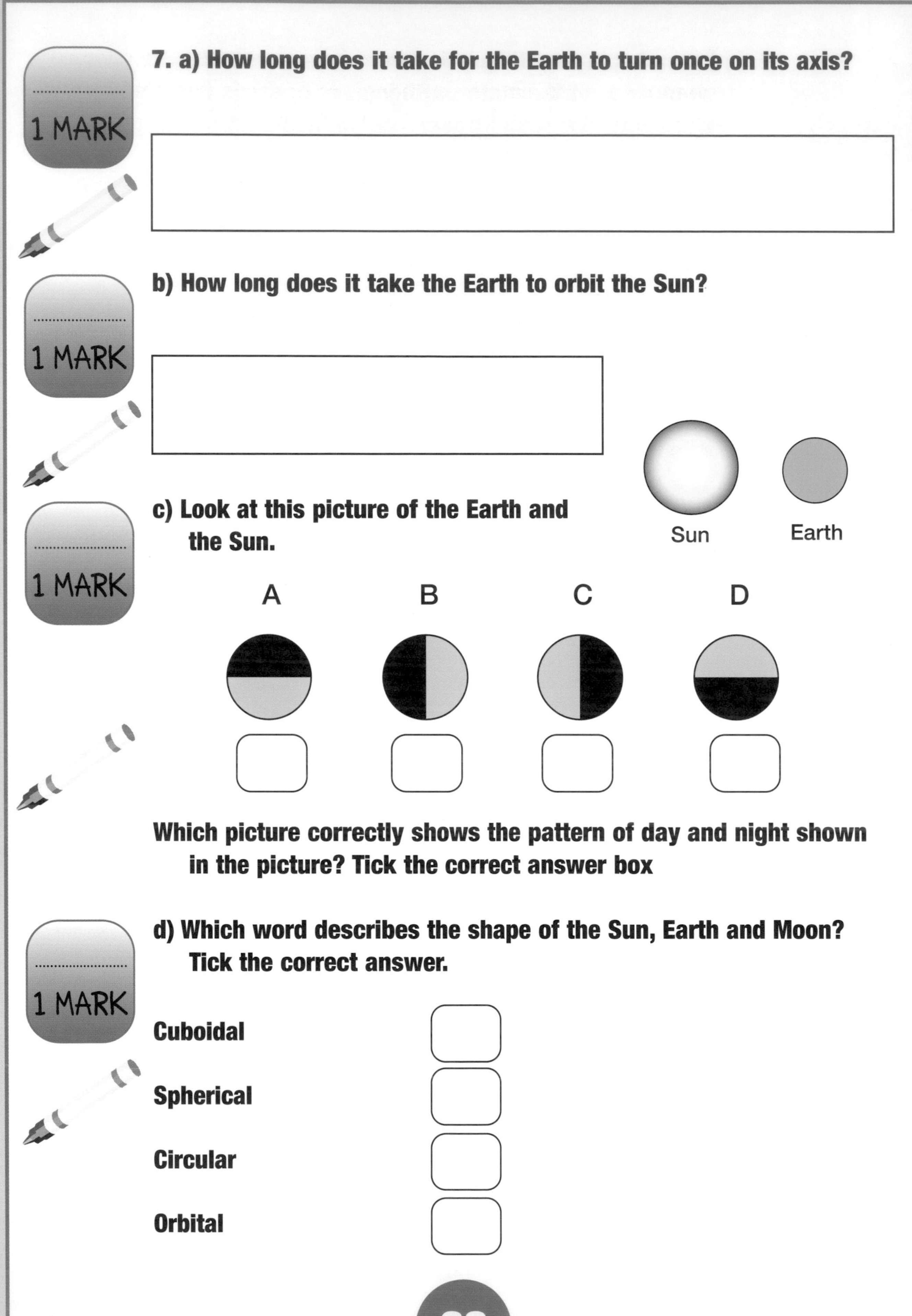

7. a) How long does it take for the Earth to turn once on its axis?

b) How long does it take the Earth to orbit the Sun?

c) Look at this picture of the Earth and the Sun.

Which picture correctly shows the pattern of day and night shown in the picture? Tick the correct answer box

d) Which word describes the shape of the Sun, Earth and Moon? Tick the correct answer.

Cuboidal

Spherical

Circular

Orbital

1 MARK

8. Chickens on Farmer Riley's farm are free-range; they are allowed to wander around, eating small insects or seeds they find on the ground. The chicken's eggs are eaten by the Riley family.

a) What is the correct term to describe this sequence of events? Tick the correct answer.

Life-cycle ☐

Food Chain ☐

Evolution ☐

1 MARK

b) The cows on the farm eat grass. The cows produce milk that is sold by Farmer Riley to the dairy. Which one of these things is a producer? Tick the correct answer.

Cow ☐

Grass ☐

Farmer Riley ☐

The Dairy ☐

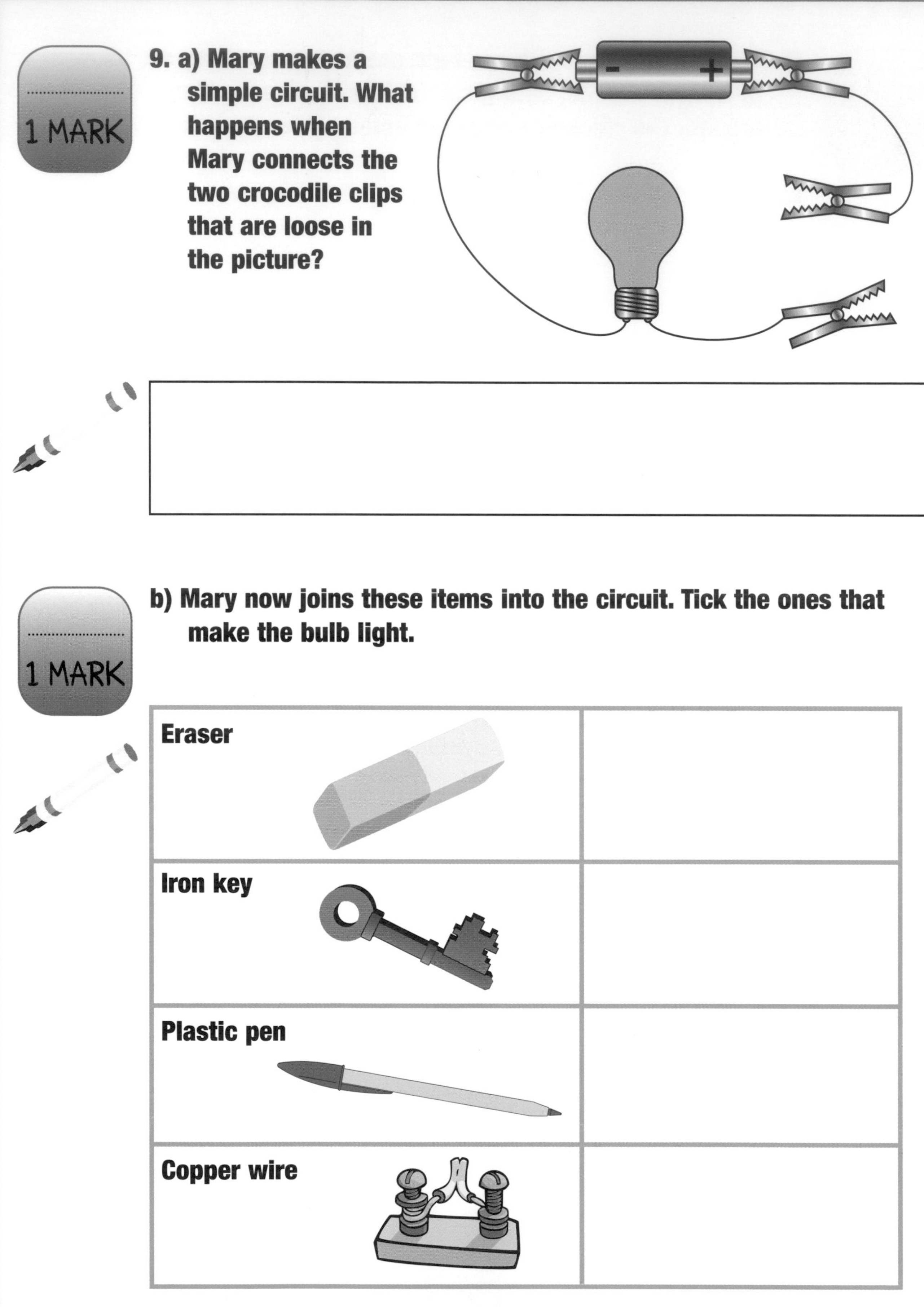

9. a) Mary makes a simple circuit. What happens when Mary connects the two crocodile clips that are loose in the picture?

b) Mary now joins these items into the circuit. Tick the ones that make the bulb light.

Item	
Eraser	
Iron key	
Plastic pen	
Copper wire	

1 MARK

c) Look at this list of materials. Sort them into the correct groups.

wood
copper
pencil lead
cork
glass
iron filings

Electrical insulators	Electrical conductors

1 MARK

d) Mary has made a simple circuit with two batteries, one switch and two bulbs. Draw a diagram of Mary's circuit. Use symbols.

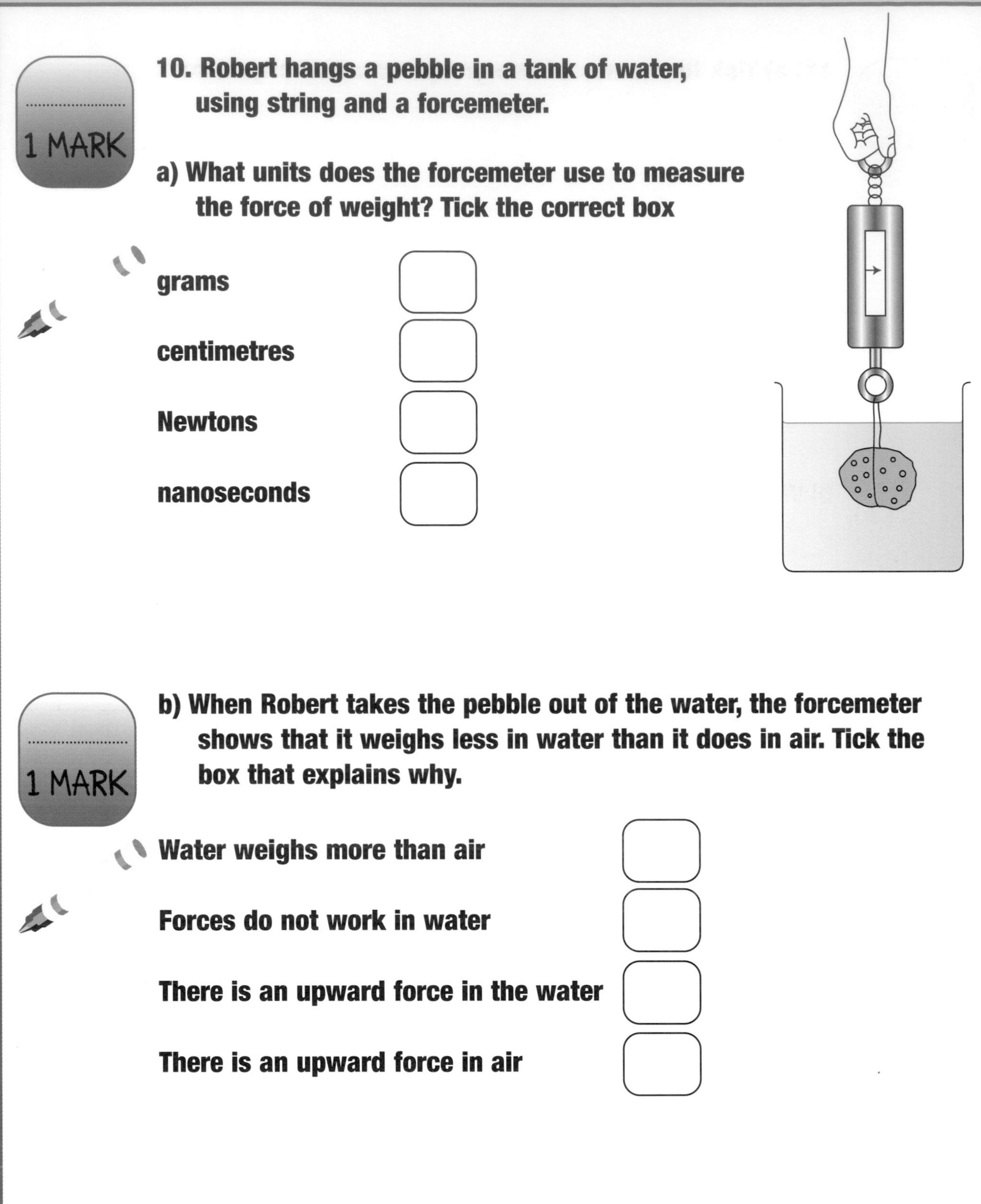

1 MARK

10. Robert hangs a pebble in a tank of water, using string and a forcemeter.

a) What units does the forcemeter use to measure the force of weight? Tick the correct box

- **grams** ☐
- **centimetres** ☐
- **Newtons** ☐
- **nanoseconds** ☐

1 MARK

b) When Robert takes the pebble out of the water, the forcemeter shows that it weighs less in water than it does in air. Tick the box that explains why.

- **Water weighs more than air** ☐
- **Forces do not work in water** ☐
- **There is an upward force in the water** ☐
- **There is an upward force in air** ☐

1 MARK

11. a) Tick the names of two groups of micro-organisms.

vertebrates	
viruses	
amphibians	
bacteria	

1 MARK

b) What is the name of the piece of equipment you would use to see micro-organisms?

2 MARKS

c) Some fungi are micro-organisms. On this table tick the statements that are true.

A. Yeast is a type of fungus that is used to make cakes and cola	
B. Yeast is a type of fungus that is used to make bread and beer	
C. Fungi make things rot, or decay	
D. Fungi cause chicken pox	
E. Fungi can make food mouldy	

Test 3
Level 6

Instructions

Read this carefully.

Answers

This shows where you will need to put your answer.

For some questions you may need to draw an answer instead of writing one.

You have 30 minutes for this test.

1. Jake and Katie are investigating some animals. They sort the animals by their characteristics.

A = Vertebrate

B = Invertebrate

C = Lays eggs

D = Gives birth to live young

E = Warm-blooded

F = Cold-blooded

1 MARK

a) Name one animal that would be in groups A, D and E.

1 MARK

b) Name one animal that would be in groups B and F.

1 MARK

c) Name two animals that would be in groups A and C.

1 MARK

d) Frogs are amphibians. Give one characteristic of an amphibian

1 MARK

2. Matter is made up of particles.

a) How are particles arranged in a gas? Tick the correct drawing.

A

B

C

b) Write true or false next to the statements below.

i) Particles in a liquid move to occupy the container.

ii) Particles in a solid vibrate slightly.

iii) Particles in a gas cannot move freely past one another.

c) An element is a pure substance. It is made of just one type of material.

A compound is made up of two or more different elements that are joined together.

A mixture is made up of two or more different elements that are not joined together.

The substances in this table are elements, compounds or mixtures. Tick a box in each row to show what each substance is.

	Element	Compound	Mixture
Air			
Carbon Dioxide			
Salt			
Gold			

3. This table shows you some items we need for good health. Link the item with its purpose in the human body. The first one has been done for you.

Water	To prevent scurvy
Fats	To make muscles
Protein	To enable blood to transport oxygen
Carbohydrates	To aid the digestive system
Iron	To dissolve soluble chemicals
Fibre	To strengthen skeleton and teeth
Calcium	To provide energy
Vitamin C	To grow nervous tissue and provide insulation

1 MARK

4. a) Look at this picture of a skier. The skier has travelled 175 metres in 10 seconds. Calculate his average speed in metres per second.

1 MARK

b) When the skier skis on one leg, how is the pressure of one ski on the snow different from the pressure of two skis?

1 MARK

c) Explain why the pressure changes in this way.

1 MARK

d) Explaln why the melted snow beneath the ski enables the skier to travel fast.

1 MARK

5. a) A fire blanket can be laid over a fire to stop it burning. Explain why this works

1 MARK

b) When coal is burned the carbon in it reacts with air. Write the equation for this.

Carbon + ... = ...

1 MARK

c) Tick the two substances that have to be present for iron to rust.

Water	Carbon	Monoxide	Oxygen	Oil

1 MARK

d) Tick the statements that are true for both burning and rusting.

They are both reversible reactions ☐

They both involve water ☐

They are both oxidations ☐

They are both chemical reactions ☐

1 MARK

6. a) Write the names of the parts of a flower labelled below.

A =

B =

C =

D =

A
B
C
D

1 MARK

b) Pollination and fertilisation are two processes necessary for the development of seeds. Describe what they involve:

i) Pollination is

ii) Fertilisation is

1 MARK

c) Explain why a germinating seed does not require light.

1 MARK

7. a) Fill in the missing words.
When a solid dissolves into water a .... is produced.

1 MARK

b) When no more solid will dissolve into the water a .... is produced.

8. Look at this picture of a food chain. Plankton is the term used to describe tiny organisms that live in the sea. They may be plants or animals.

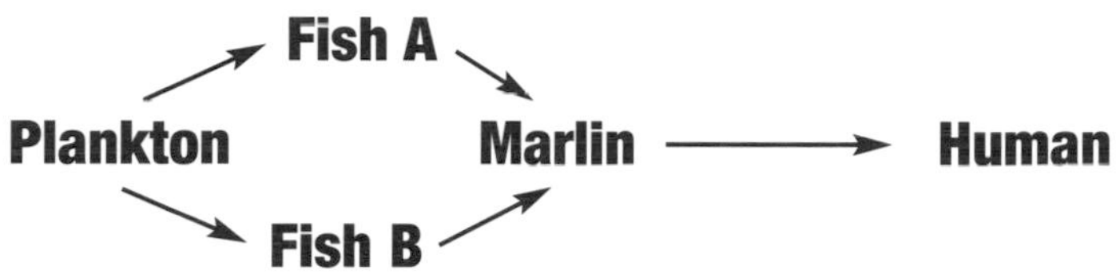

	Fish A		
Plankton ↗ ↘		Marlin →	Human
	Fish B		

Plankton → Fish A → Marlin; Plankton → Fish B → Marlin; Marlin → Human

1 MARK

a) Name the producer in this food chain.

1 MARK

b) Name the secondary consumer in this food chain.

1 MARK

c) Describe what would happen to the populations of fishes A and B if humans hunted and caught a noticeably larger number of marlin, and why.

1 MARK

d) Some whales depend upon plankton as a source of food. Describe what might happen to their population if there are fewer marlins after extensive hunting by humans, and why.

Test 1

Answers and Marking Scheme

1.

	Yes	No
Raw Egg ⇒ Fried Egg		✓
Wood ⇒ Ash		✓
Water ⇒ Steam	✓	
Dough ⇒ Bread		✓

Award two marks for four correct answers. Award one mark for three correct answers.

2. a) Crocodile = river; squirrel = tree; ant = soil. Award 1 mark for all three correct answers.

b) Accept any features that are suitable as long as the way the feature helps is clear and accurate, e.g. hump for storing fat and water, long eyelashes to keep sand out of its eyes, broad feet to walk on sand, etc.

3. a) For one mark the word 'absorbent' must be used.

b) Waterproof
Award one mark.

c) Condensation
Award one mark.

d) When I put water in the kettle it is a liquid. When it boils it turns into a gas. When I put water into the freezer it turns into ice, which is a solid.
Award one mark.

e) Transparent
Award one mark.

4. a)

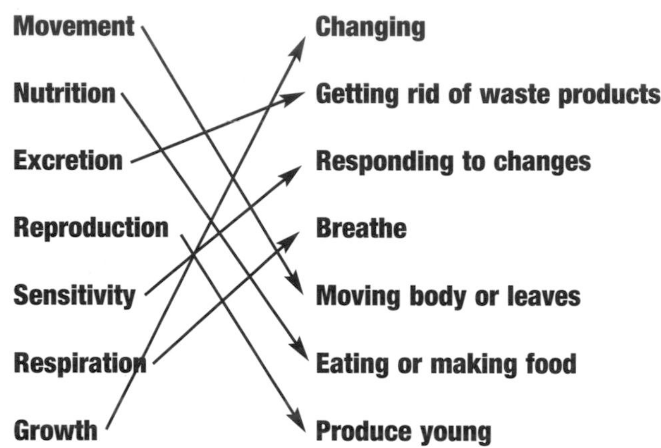

Award one mark.

b) Cotton jumper, cork, book all need to be ticked for one mark.

5. a)

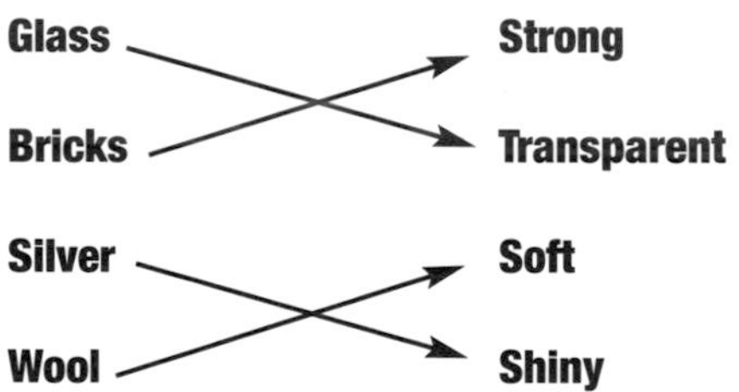

Award one mark.

b) Explanation must include the fact that metal conducts electricity.
Award one mark.

c) Explanation must include the fact that plastic does not conduct electricity (an insulator).
Award one mark.

d) For one mark circles must be placed over both plastic and polystyrene.

6. a)
A = Flower Petals
B = Stem
C = Leaf
D = Root
All four must be correct for one mark.

b) Any combination of three of these answers is acceptable for one mark:
By animals eating them
By getting caught in animals fur
By wind
By exploding pods

c) Explanation must mention that the plant needed sunlight, for one mark.

d) Gas to live = carbon dioxide
Gas produced as a waste produce = oxygen
The gases must be in the correct order for one mark

7. a) 5
b) 4
c) 3
d) Explanation must include the fact that the blood passing through the vessels is the pulse. Mention must be made of the heart beating or pumping.
Award one mark for each correct answer.

8. a) Baked potato; milk; apple
All three must be correct for one mark.

b) Award one mark for two correct suggestions, two marks for three correct suggestions from this list:
Visit the dentist regularly/have check-ups
Avoid sugary food
Avoid sugary/fizzy drinks
Brush teeth twice a day
Eat food with calcium

c) It helps the digestive system
Award one mark.

9. a) Magnet
Award one mark.

b) Filter
Award one mark.

c) It has dissolved
Award one mark.

d) He left it to dry/heated it so the water could evaporate/turn into a gas/vapour
Award one mark.

10. a) Midday
Award one mark.

b) The explanation should include the fact that the cloud has passed in front of the Sun, blocking out the light. (one mark) Everything around Linda will have been put in to shadow (one mark).

c) It is night-time in Australia when it is daytime here.
Award one mark.

Test 2 Answers and Marking Scheme

1. a) Beetle and sparrow
Award one mark for both correct answers.

b) Beetle and millipede
Award one mark for both correct answers.

c) B, C and E must be circled for two marks, two must be circled correctly for one mark.

2. a) Television, lamp and Sun must all be ticked for one mark.

b)

Material	Some light passes through	No light passes through
Cardboard		✓
Diamond	✓	
Clear plastic	✓	
Tissue paper	✓	
Mirror		✓

Award one mark.

c) Television and fire must both be ticked for two marks.

d) They are light sources
Award one mark for both correct answers.

3. a) Tooth A has two roots, Tooth B has one root
Tooth A is rounded, Tooth B is sharp
Award one mark for either of these differences.

b) They have different functions
Award one mark.

c) Tooth B
Award one mark.

d) Tooth A
Award one mark.

4. a) The jelly cubes dissolve
Award one mark.

b) No
Award one mark.

c) Stir the mixture
Award one mark.

d) The particles are tightly packed together
Award one mark.

5. a) Petal – attracts insects; Fruit – helps distribute seeds; Roots – Take in water; Leaves – Take in carbon dioxide; Shoot – Transports water
Award two marks for all correct answers, one mark for three or four correct answers

b) 1 = Pollination; 2 = Germination; 3 = Seed dispersal
Award one mark for one or two out of three correct, two marks for all correct.

6. a) Air
Award one mark.

b) How high or low a note is
Award one mark.

c) It gets higher
Award one mark.

d) It gets higher
Award one mark.

7. a) 24 hours or one day
Award one mark.

b) Accept 365 or 366 days or anything in between.
Award one mark.

c) C
Award one mark.

d) Spherical
Award one mark.

8. a) Food chain
Award one mark.

b) Grass
Award one mark.

9. a) The bulb lights up
Award one mark.

b) Iron key and copper wire
Both must be ticked for one mark – no mark if either of the other options have a tick).

c) electrical insulators = wood, cork and glass
electrical conductors = pencil lead, iron filings and copper
Award one mark.

d) One mark for all components shown correctly.
Switch may be open or closed.

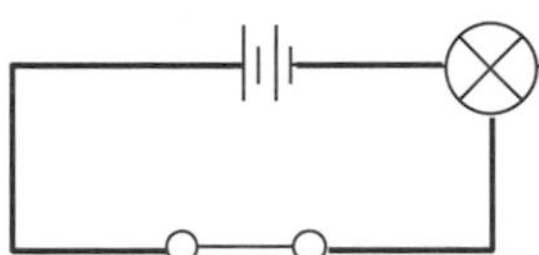

10. a) Newtons
Award one mark.

b) There is an upward force in the water
Award one mark.

11. a) Viruses and bacteria alone should be ticked for one mark.

b) Microscope
Award one mark.

c) B, C and E must all be ticked, and none others, for two marks. If two correct answers are ticked award one mark.

Test 3
Answers and Marking Scheme

1. a) Tiger or dolphin
Award one mark.

b) Octopus
Award one mark.

c) Snake, lizard, eagle, frog
Award one mark.

d) Moist skin; can breathe in water or air; lays eggs in water; has a life-cycle that includes a tadpole stage
Award one mark for any of the above.

2. a) C
Award one mark.

b) i) True; ii) True; iii) False
Award one mark if all three parts are answered correctly.

c)

	Element	Compound	Mixture
Air			✓
Carbon Dioxide		✓	
Salt		✓	
Gold	✓		

Award one mark for three correct answers, two marks for four correct answers.

3.

Water	To prevent scurvy
Fats	To make muscles
Protein	To enable blood to transport oxygen
Carbohydrates	To aid the digestive system
Iron	To dissolve soluble chemicals
Fibre	To strengthen skeleton and teeth
Calcium	To provide energy
Vitamin C	To grow nervous tissue and provide insulation

Award four marks for all correct; three marks for six correct; two marks for four correct; one mark for two correct.

4. a) 17.5 m
Award one mark.

b) The pressure is increased
Award one mark.

c) Award one mark for description that includes the fact that a greater weight is being put on a smaller area.

d) For one mark it must be stated that the water acts as a lubricant (or similar word) to reduce friction.

5. a) The blanket prevents air from getting to the fire
Award one mark.

b) Carbon + Oxygen → Carbon Dioxide (accept chemical symbols instead of words)
Award one mark.

c) Water and oxygen must both be ticked for one mark.

d) They are both oxidations and they are both chemical reactions.
Both must be ticked for one mark.

6. a) A = Stamen; B = Carpel; C = Sepal; D = Petal
All four must be correct for one mark.

b) i) Pollination is the process by which pollen lands on the sticky stigma.
Award one mark (mention of the stigma being sticky is not essential).

ii) Fertilisation is when the pollen grain (accept male sex cell) joins with the egg (accept ovule or female sex cell).
Award one mark.

c) Germinating seeds do not require light because they contain their own food supply.
Award one mark.

7. a) Solution
Award one mark.

b) Saturated solution
Award one mark.

8. a) Plankton
Award one mark.

b) Marlin
Award one mark.

c) Without marlins being able to predate on them, populations of Fish A and Fish B would increase.
Award one mark.

d) Once the marlin numbers are reduced the populations of Fish A and Fish B will thrive. Greater numbers of Fish A and Fish B will eat more plankton, leaving less for the whales. The whale population could be expected to decrease.
Award one mark for any explanation that says the whale numbers will be fewer because they will have less food.

Answers: Revision Section

Page 6
1. No
2. No
3. Oxygen

Page 7
1. True
2. False
3. True

Page 8
1. Wood, feathers, flour and rubber

Page 9
1. They all have the Seven Life Processes
2. Plants make their own food, they move slowly, they keep growing and they do not communicate
3. Cells

Page 10
1. Dogs, wolves, bears, cats, etc.
2. Cows, goats, sheep, rabbits, etc.
3. True

Page 11
1. Milk
2. Sugar
3. No. Too much is bad for you, but you do need it small amounts.

Page 12
1. True
2. False

Page 13
1. Skull
2. Heart and lungs
3. True

Page 14
1. Talk, walk
2. When the male sperm joins to the female egg

Page 15
1. False
2. False
3. False

Page 16
1. Flower
2. Respiration – taking in carbon dioxide and turning it into food with water and sunlight
3. To anchor them to the ground and to take up water

Page 17
1. a) It would die; b) It would die
2. Oxygen

Page 18
1. When pollen reaches the stigma
2. Female

Page 19
1. When a seed begins to grow
2. Ovary
3. By animals, wind or pod explosion

Page 20
1. Group 1: salmon, trout, cod – all fish. They swim, have streamlined bodies, have scales etc.
Group 2: goat, camel, cow – all are grazing animals
Group 3: snail, ant, worm – none of these have backbones, they all live in soil or under stones and plants

Page 21
1. Reptiles
2. Fish
3. Mammals

Page 22
1. Animals that eat plants
2. Animals that hunt other animals for food

Page 23
1. For making bread and beer, to rot and decay dead things
2. Measles, chicken pox, foot and mouth etc.
3. To remove harmful micro-organisms

Page 24
1. Rocks under the ground
2. It has a liquid state

Page 25
1. True
2. True, but salty water conducts it better
3. True

Page 26
1. False
2. True
3. False

Page 27
1. A mixture of water and a soluble solid
2. Salt, sugar, coffee granules, aspirin
3. The air puts bubbles into the water

Page 28
1. Using a sieve
2. Using a filter

Page 29
1. When a liquid becomes a vapour or gas
2. A mixture of a soluble solid and water
3. A solid that will not dissolve in water

Page 30
1. Because it is an electrical insulator
2. Because the circuits are not complete

Page 31
1. True
2. True
3. False

Page 32
1. Push and pull (repel and attract)
2. It will have no effect

Page 33
1. 3 Newtons
2. A
3. Unbalanced

Page 34
1. False
2. False

Page 35
1. How high or low a note is
2. It vibrates the medium (e.g. air) and the vibrations are passed on to our ears
3. True

Page 36
1. A path or journey around another body, e.g. the Sun
2. 365 (and a bit!)

Page 37
1. Midday (noon)
2. East
3. No

Glossary

Here are some important words you should try and learn before your test. Cover up the words and test yourself on the meanings.

Amplitude
How loud a sound is.
Anther
The top of a stamen (male part of the flower) – it has the pollen on it.
Artery
A blood vessel that takes blood with oxygen to parts of the body.
Bacteria
Types of micro-organism.
Battery
A source of energy.
Biceps
The large muscles at the top of your arm.
Canine teeth
Sharp, fang-like teeth.
Carbohydrates
Foods that supply fast energy.
Carnivore
An animal that eats meat.
Cells
The building blocks of all life.
Circulatory system
A network of blood vessels and a heart.
Classification
A system for putting living things into groups.
Condensation
When a gas turns into a vapour after cooling.
Conductor
A thermal conductor passes heat on, an electrical conductor passes electricity on.
Decibels
The unit that sound is measured in.
Electricity
A source of energy that is carried by wires and stored in batteries.
Environment
The place and surroundings in which an animal or plant lives.
Evaporation
The change from liquid to gas, often after heat is applied.
Fats
Foods that supply slow energy.
Fertilisation
When a male sex cell and a female sex cell join to form a new life.
Fibre
A type of food that is hard to digest; it helps the digestive system work properly.
Filtration
A way of separating a liquid and an insoluble solid using a filter.
Food chain
Used to describe how plants and animals may depend on one another for food.
Friction
A force that slows things down when they are rubbed together.
Fungus
A type of living organism that is plant-like but does not make its own food using sunlight.
Germinate
When a seed begins to grow.
Gravity
A force that pulls things towards the centre of the Earth.
Habitat
The place where an animal or plant lives.
Herbivore
A plant-eating animal.
Igneous rock
Rock made when molten rock from below the Earth's surface cools.
Incisor
Sharp front teeth.
Insoluble
Solids that do not dissolve in water.
Irreversible change
A change that can not be undone.
Life-cycle
A description of the changes that an organism undergoes throughout its life.
Mass
The amount of matter contained in something.
Metamorphic rock
A rock that has been changed by great heat or pressure.
Metamorphosis
A change in body shape.
Micro-organism
An organism that is too small to be seen with the naked eye.
Molars
Back teeth used for grinding food.
Nutrients
Substances in food or soil that are essential for healthy growth.
Opaque
Does not let light through.
Orbit
The journey or path followed by a planet, asteroid or moon around another planet or star.
Organism
A living thing.
Ovary
Contains eggs.
Ovule
Egg.
Petal
The brightly coloured part of a flower.
Photosynthesis
The process by which plants use sunlight to turn water and carbon dioxide into energy and oxygen.
Plaque
The sticky substance that forms on teeth as a result of bacteria feeding on sugar.
Plasma
The liquid part of blood – it contains the blood cells.
Platelets
Blood cells that form scabs and make blood clot.
Pliable
Used to describe bendy materials.
Pollination
The process by which pollen is transferred from the male part of the plant to the female part.
Predators
Animals that hunt others for food.
Producers
Organisms at the beginning of a food chain.
Proteins
Foods that help bodies grow and repair.
Pulse
The beating of blood in a wrist.
Red cells
Blood cells that carry oxygen around your body.
Reflection
When light is bounced off a surface.
Reversible change
A change to a material that can be undone.
Root
The part of the plant that is in the soil, takes up water and anchors the plant.
Sedimentary rock
A rock that is formed by pressure and time acting on layers of soil or mud deposits.
Seed dispersal
The way seeds travel away from the parent plant.
Shadow
An absence of light caused when a light source is blocked.
Soluble
A solid that dissolves.
Source of light
Something that gives out light rather than reflecting it.
Species
A group of animals that breed with one another.
Stamen
The male part of the flower.
States of matter
Terms that describe the physical formation of a material, e.g. solid, liquid or gas.
Stigma
The tip of the female part of a flower; it is often sticky so pollen adheres to it.
Transparent
See-through.
Triceps
The muscles on the underside of your arm.
Veins
Blood vessels that carry blood without oxygen back to your heart.
Vibration
A fast shaking forwards and backwards.
Virus
A type of micro-organism.
Water vapour
Water that has changed into a gas; also called steam.
White cells
Blood cells that fight infection.